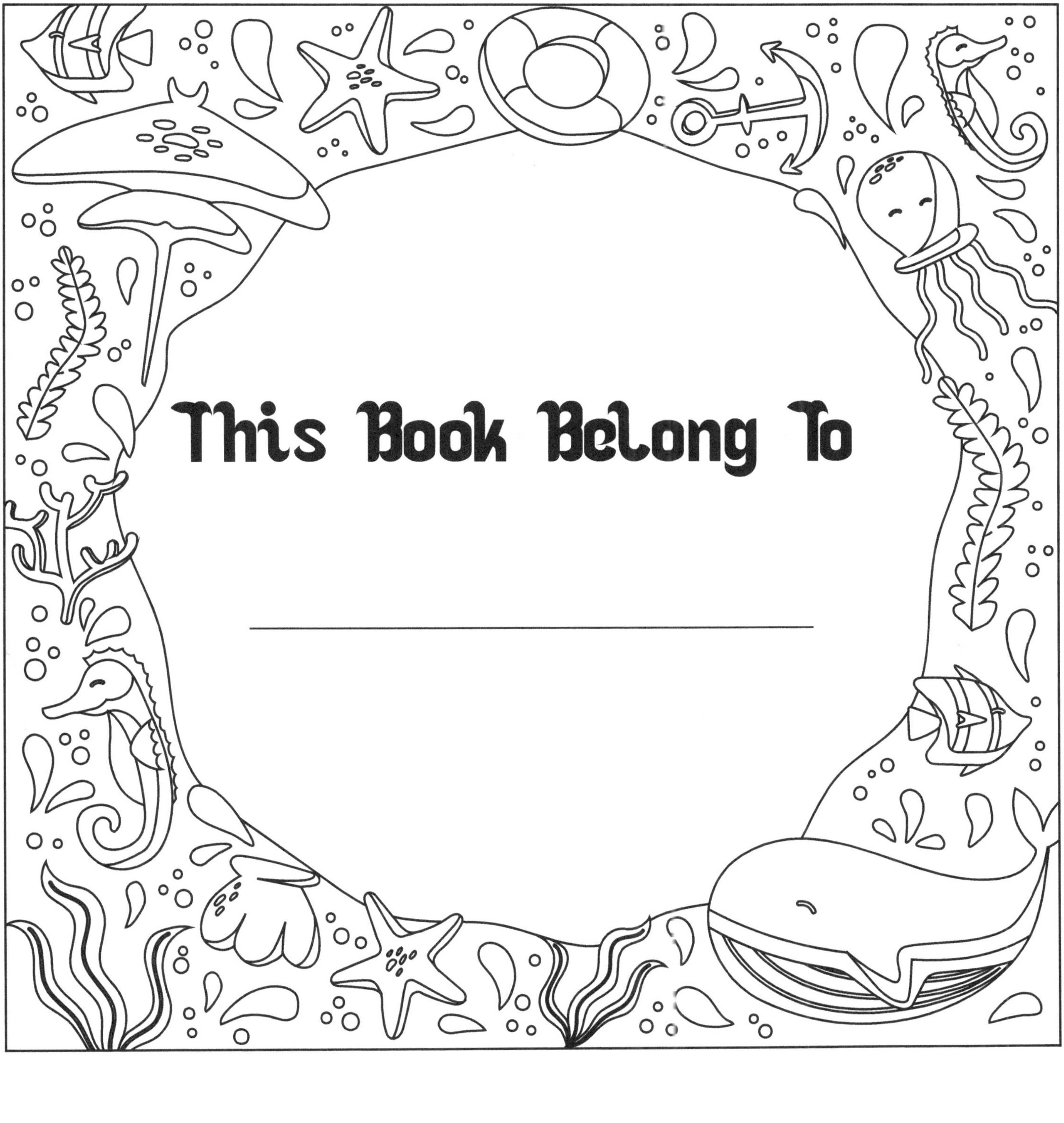

This Book Belong To

_____

ABOUT THIS BOOK

Thank you for purchasing this quality coloring book from Sunrise Coloring!

Inside this book are 40 unique and fun Coral Reef coloring pages designed especially for kids.

Each image is on its own page with a BLANK backside to help avoid color bleed-through if you color with markers or other ink based pens.

If you use something other than colored pencils or crayons, we also recom-mend placing a sheet of paper or some other blotter between your coloring page and the one beneath it while you work.

We hope you enjoy your Coral Reef Coloring Book!

TEST COLOR PAGE

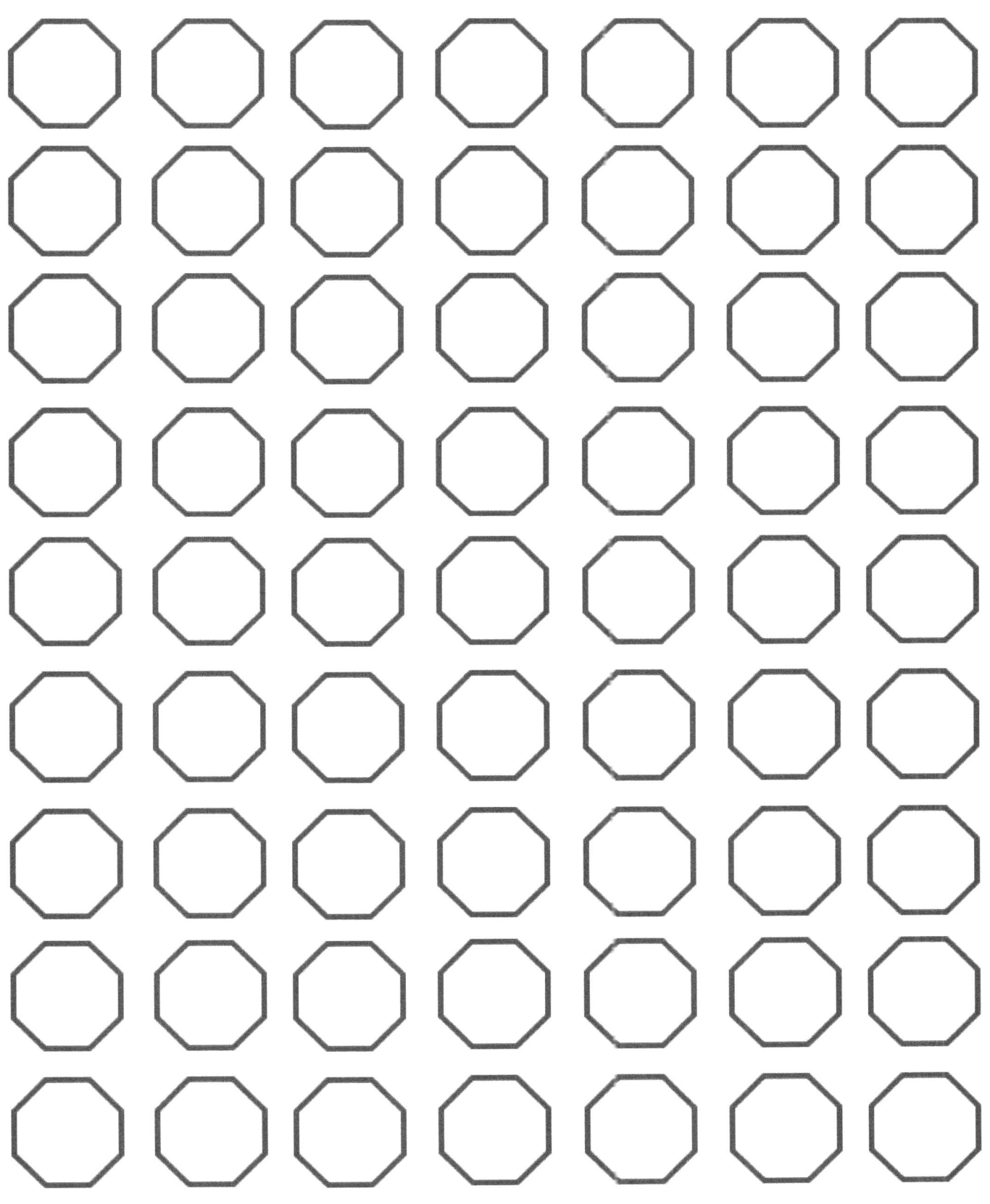

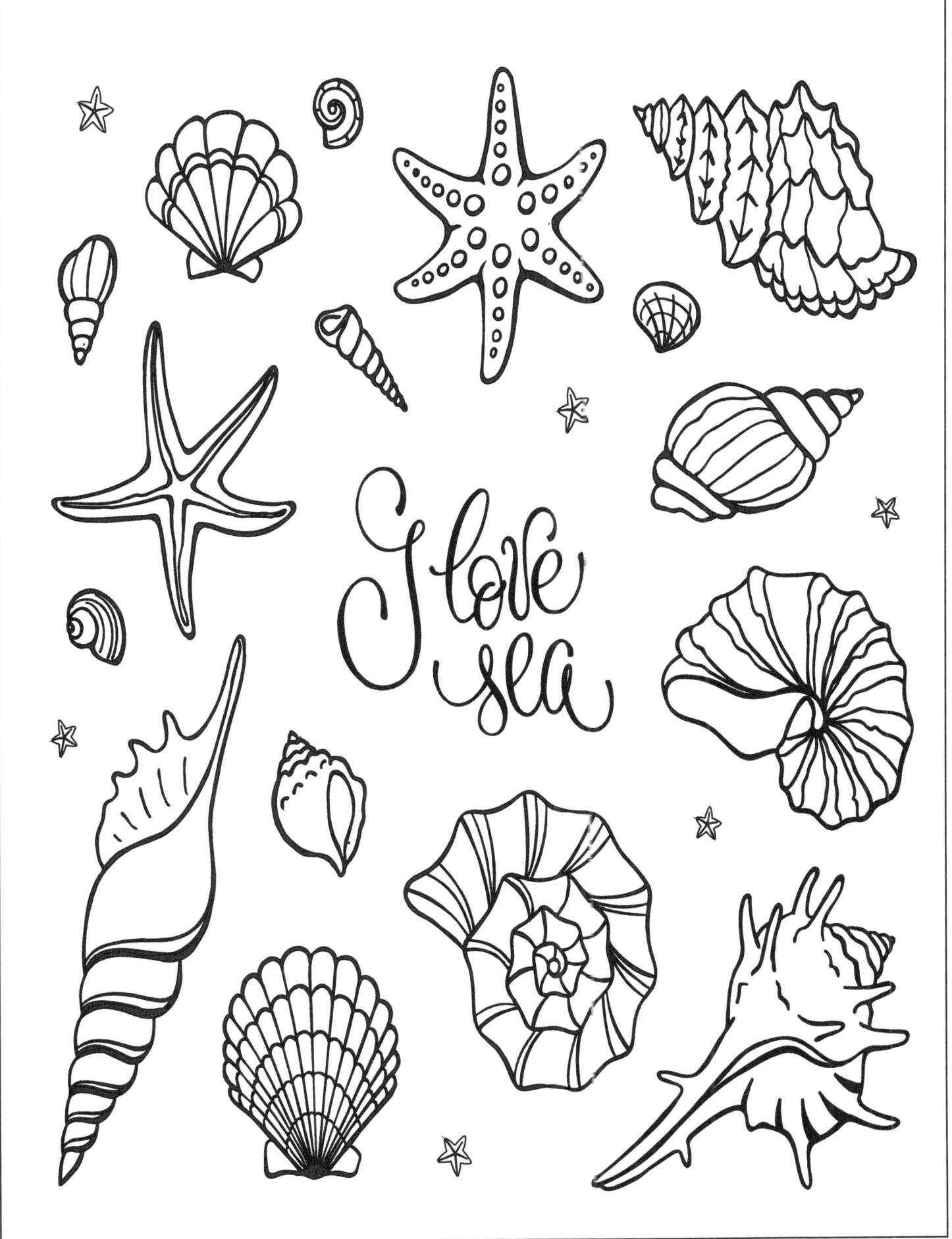

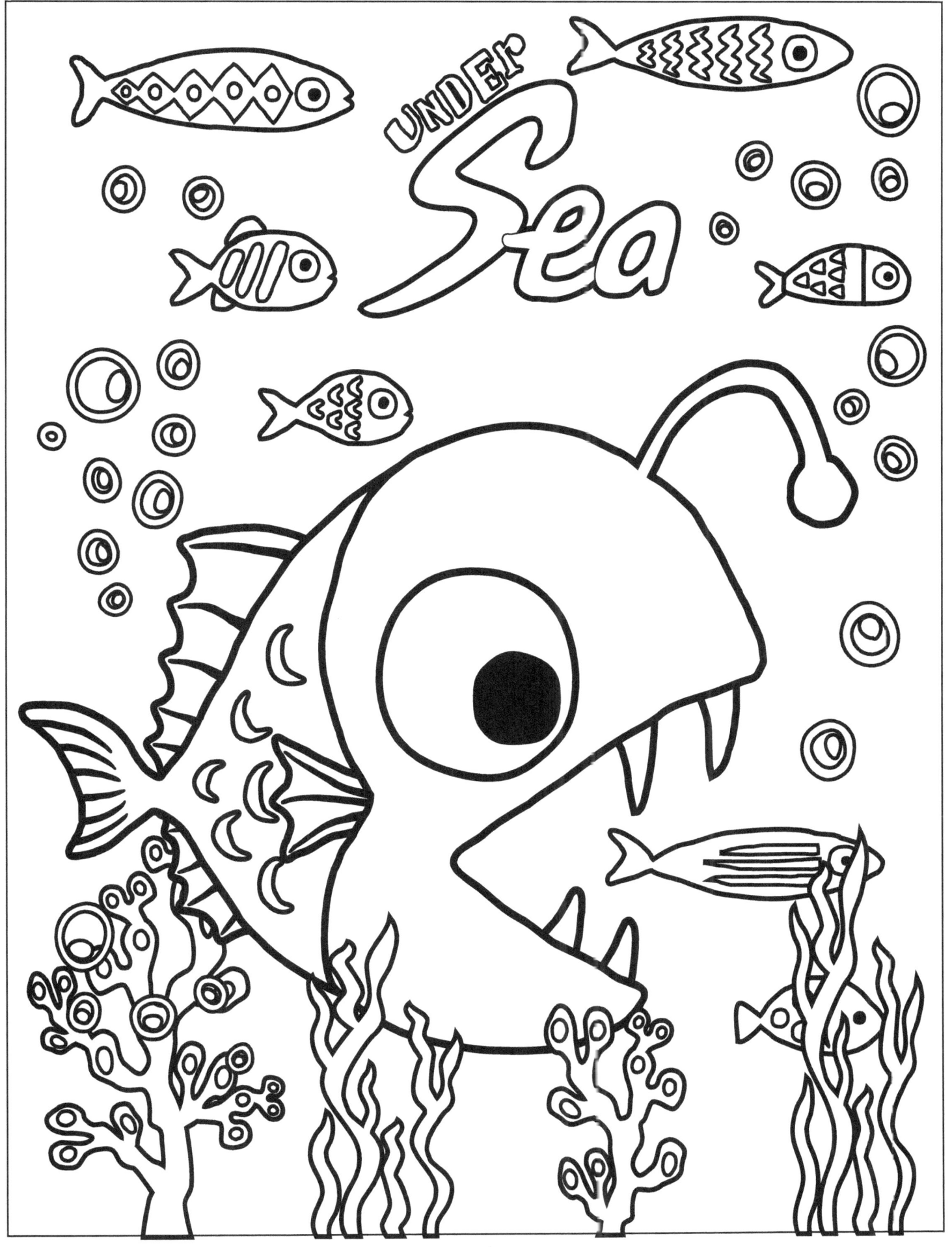

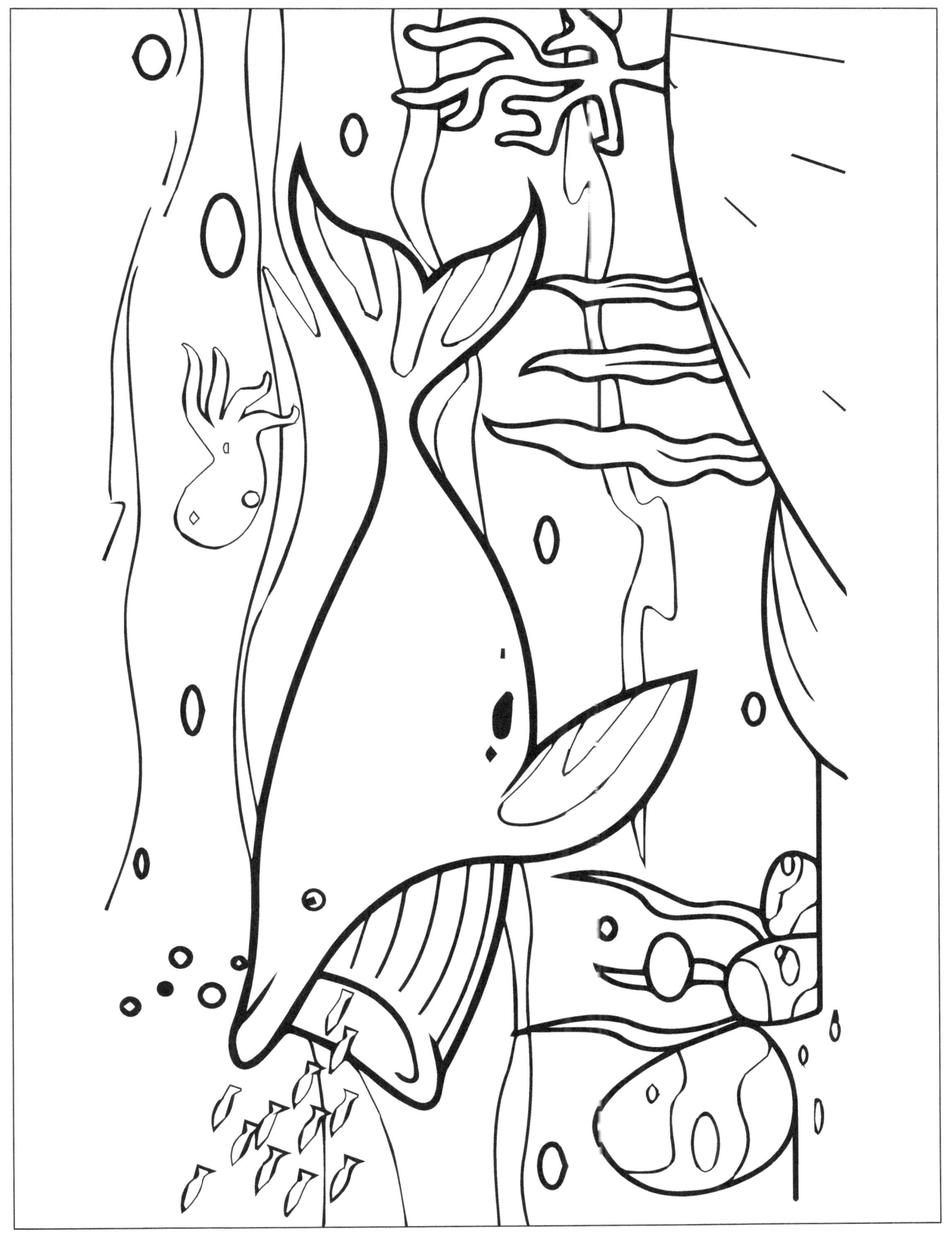

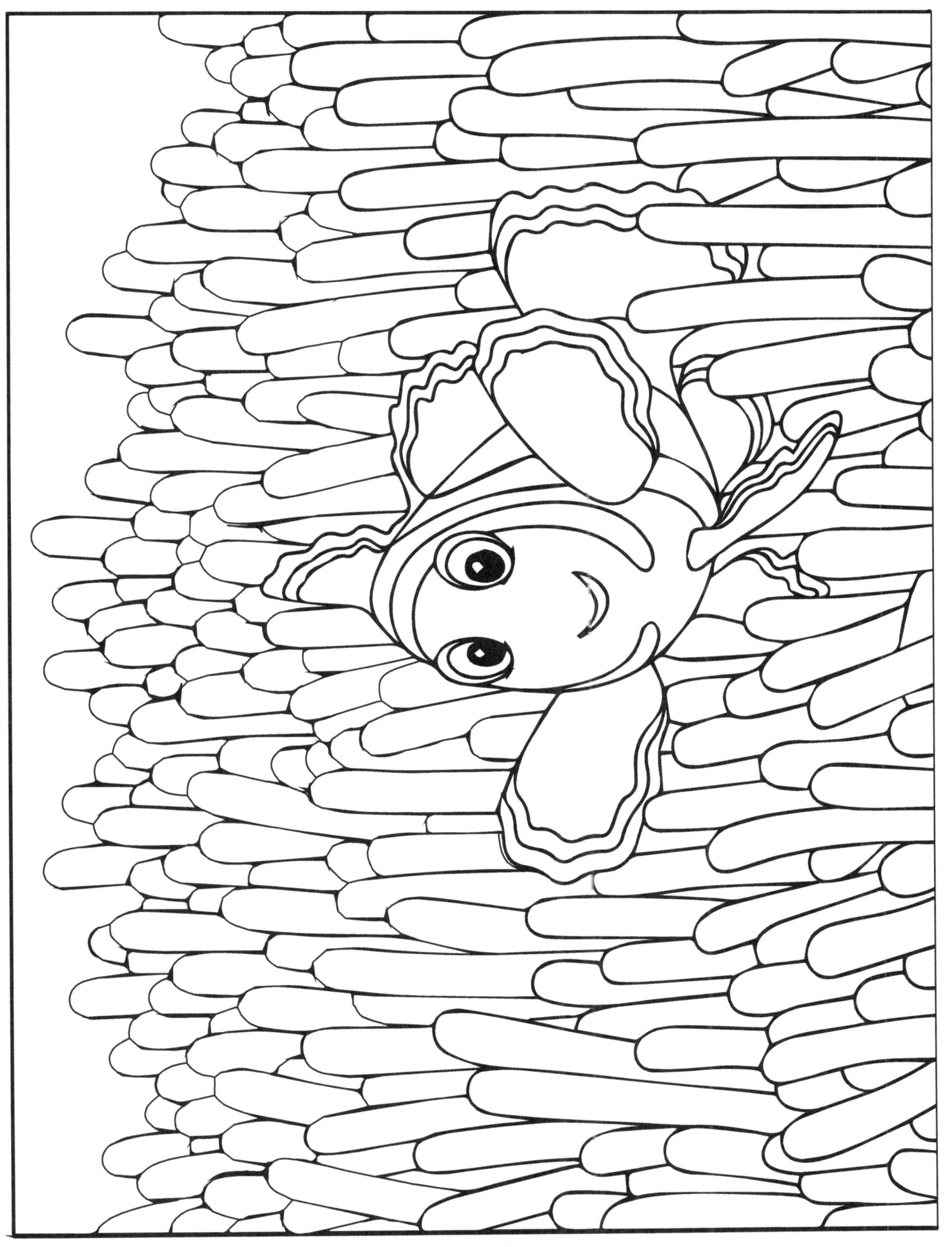

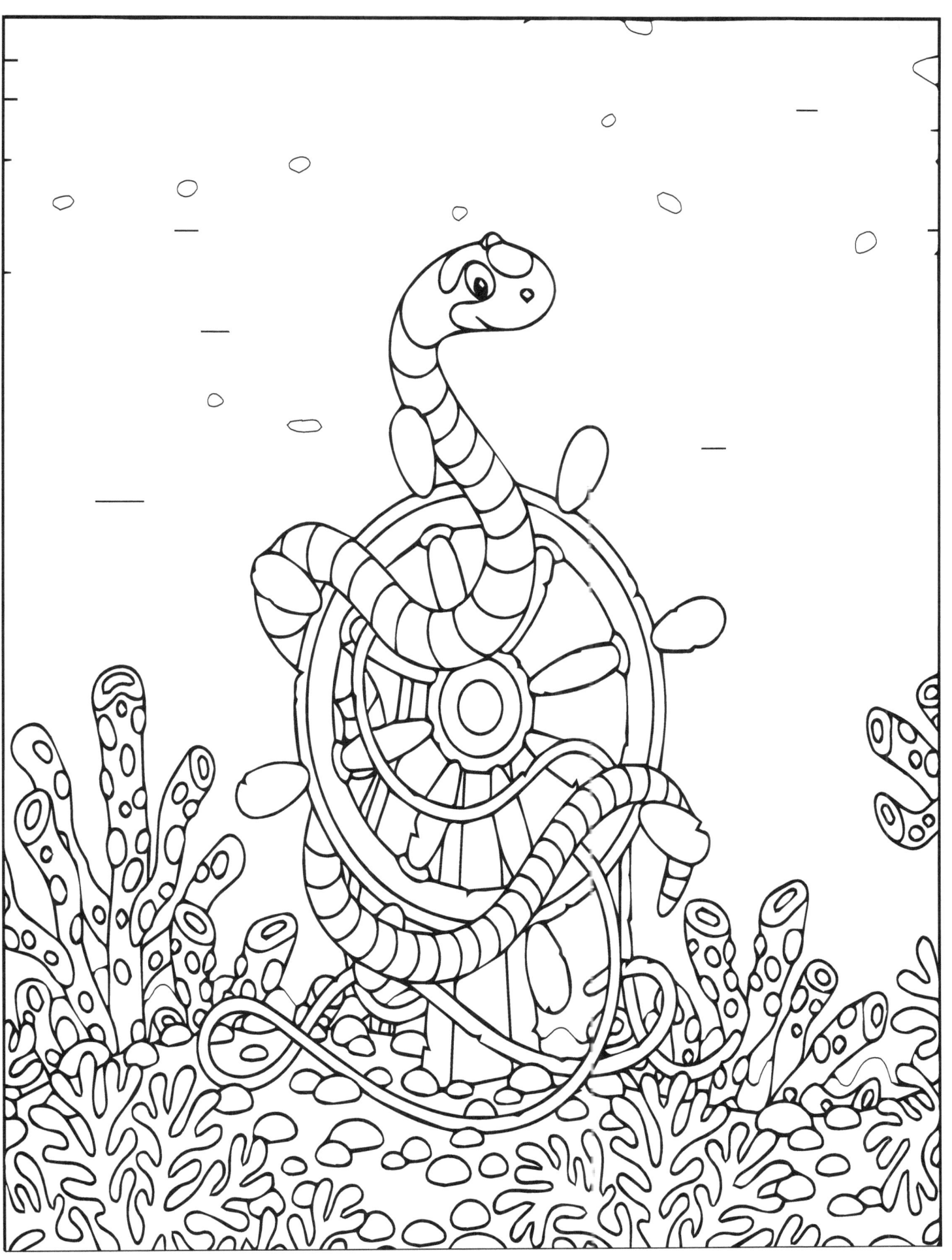

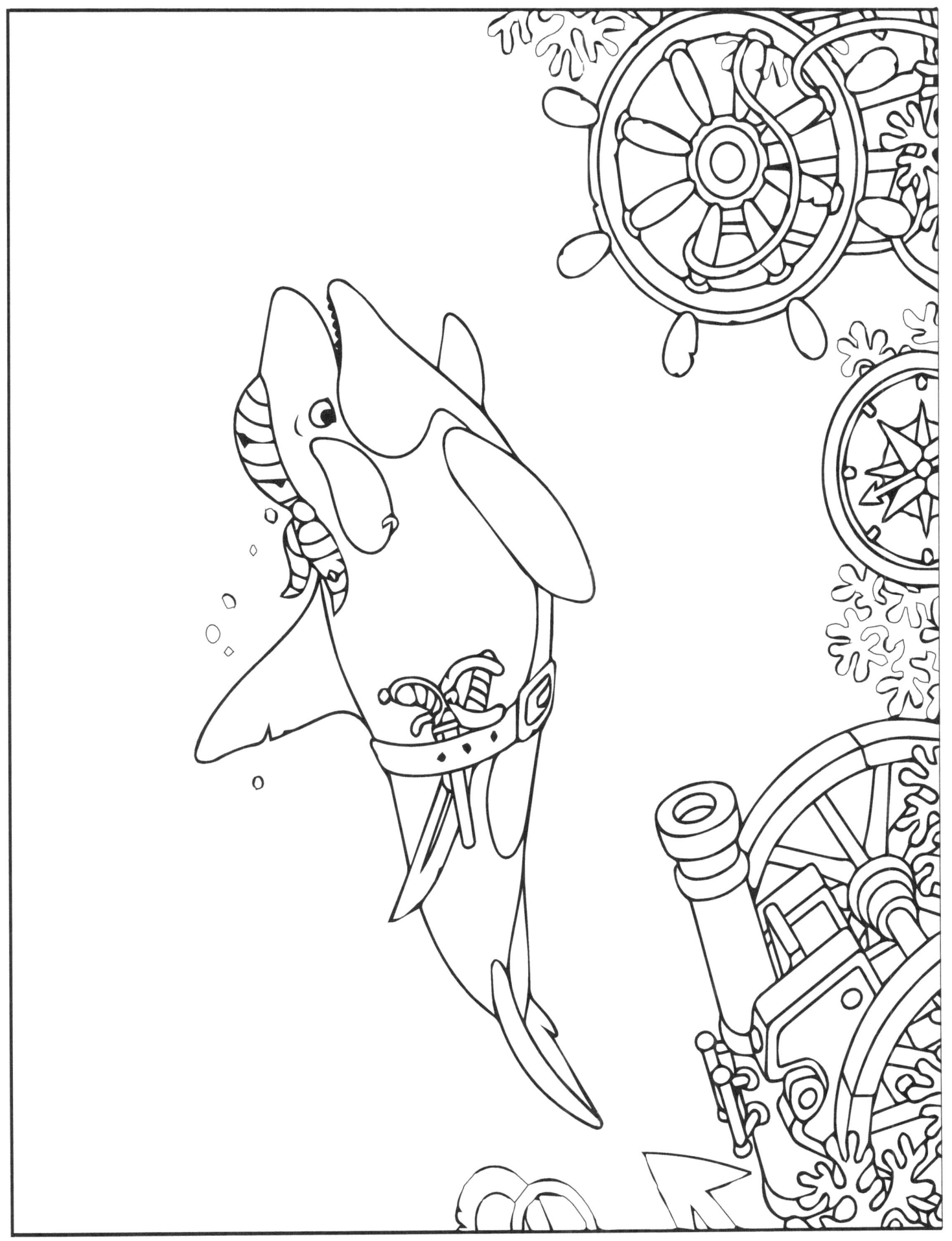

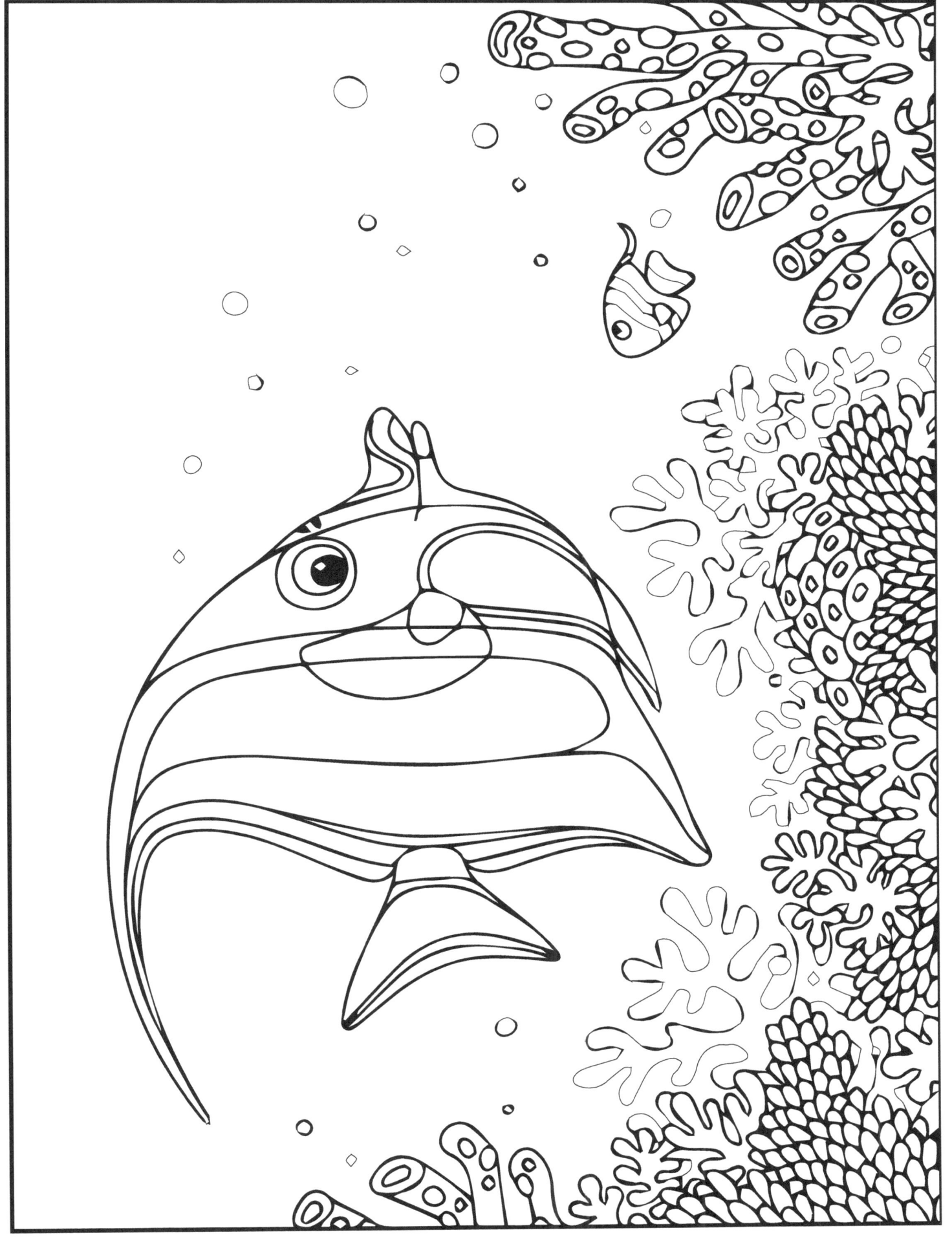

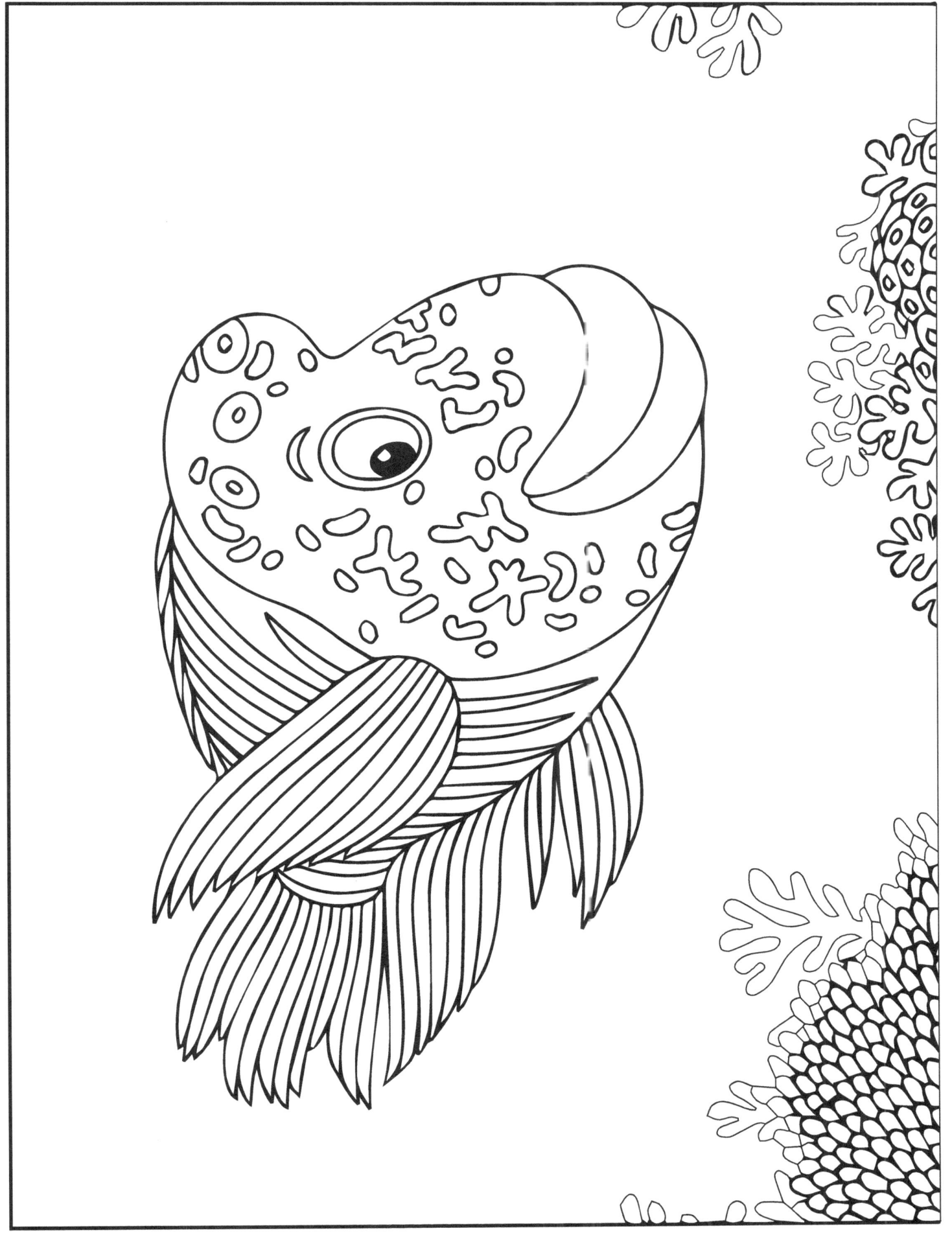

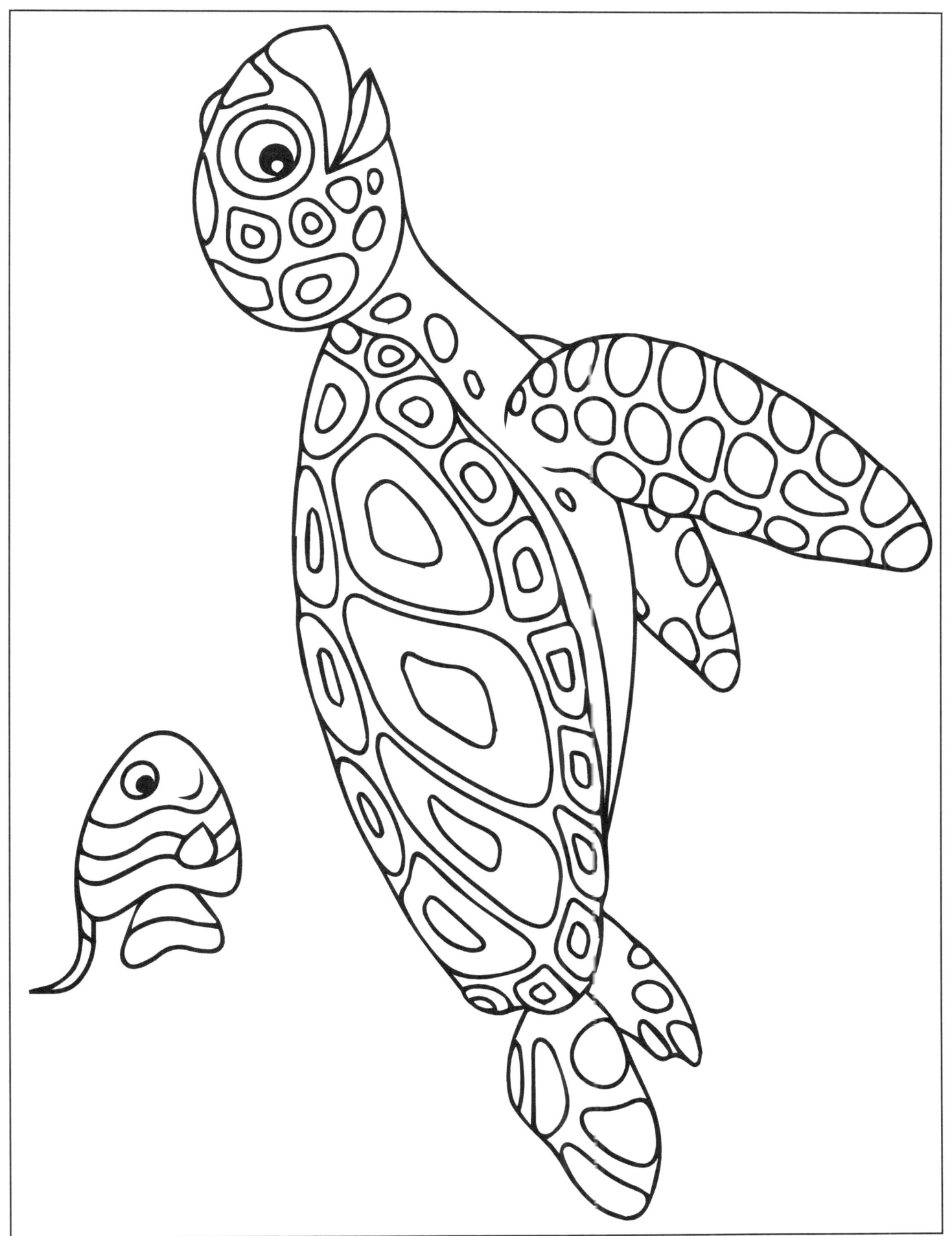

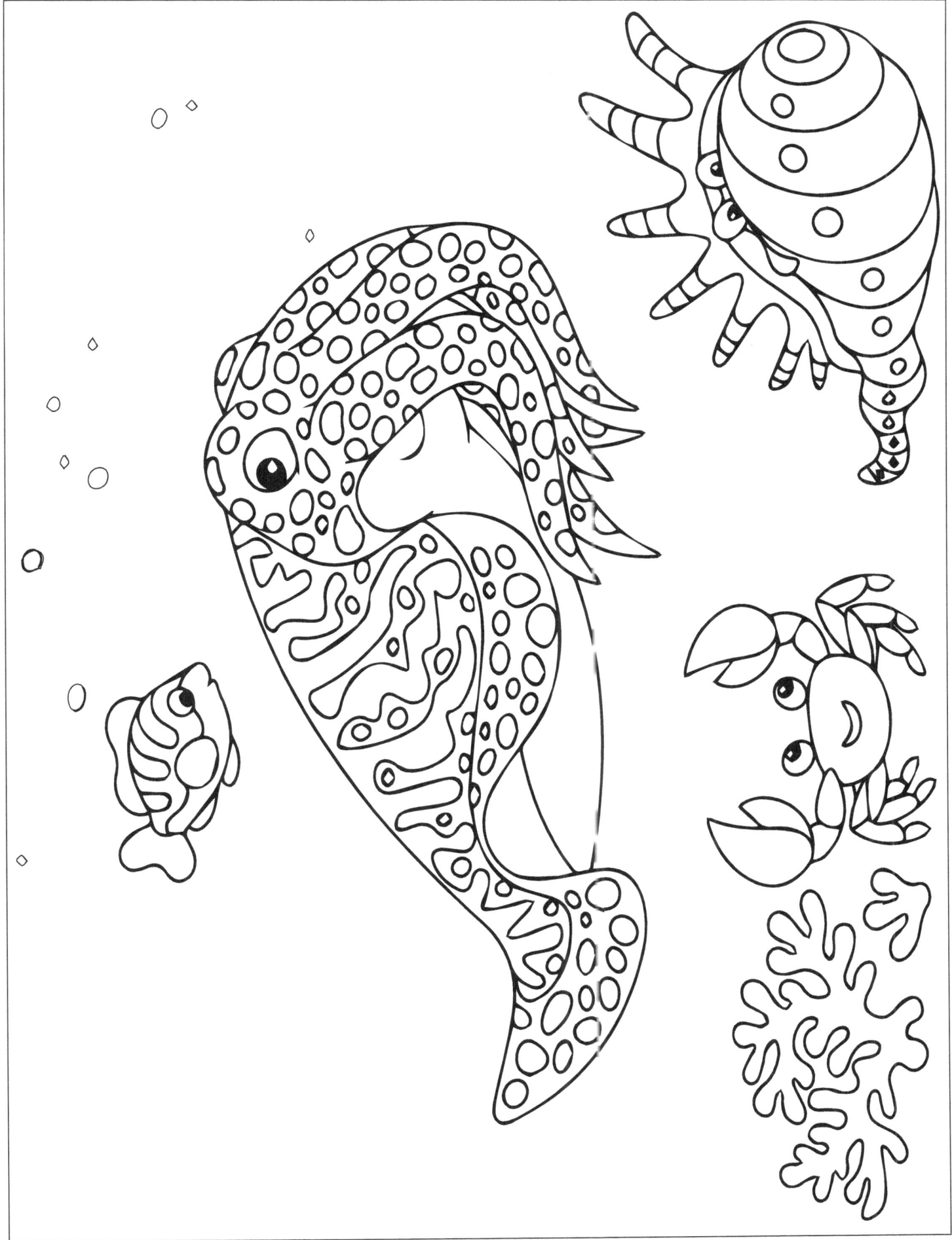

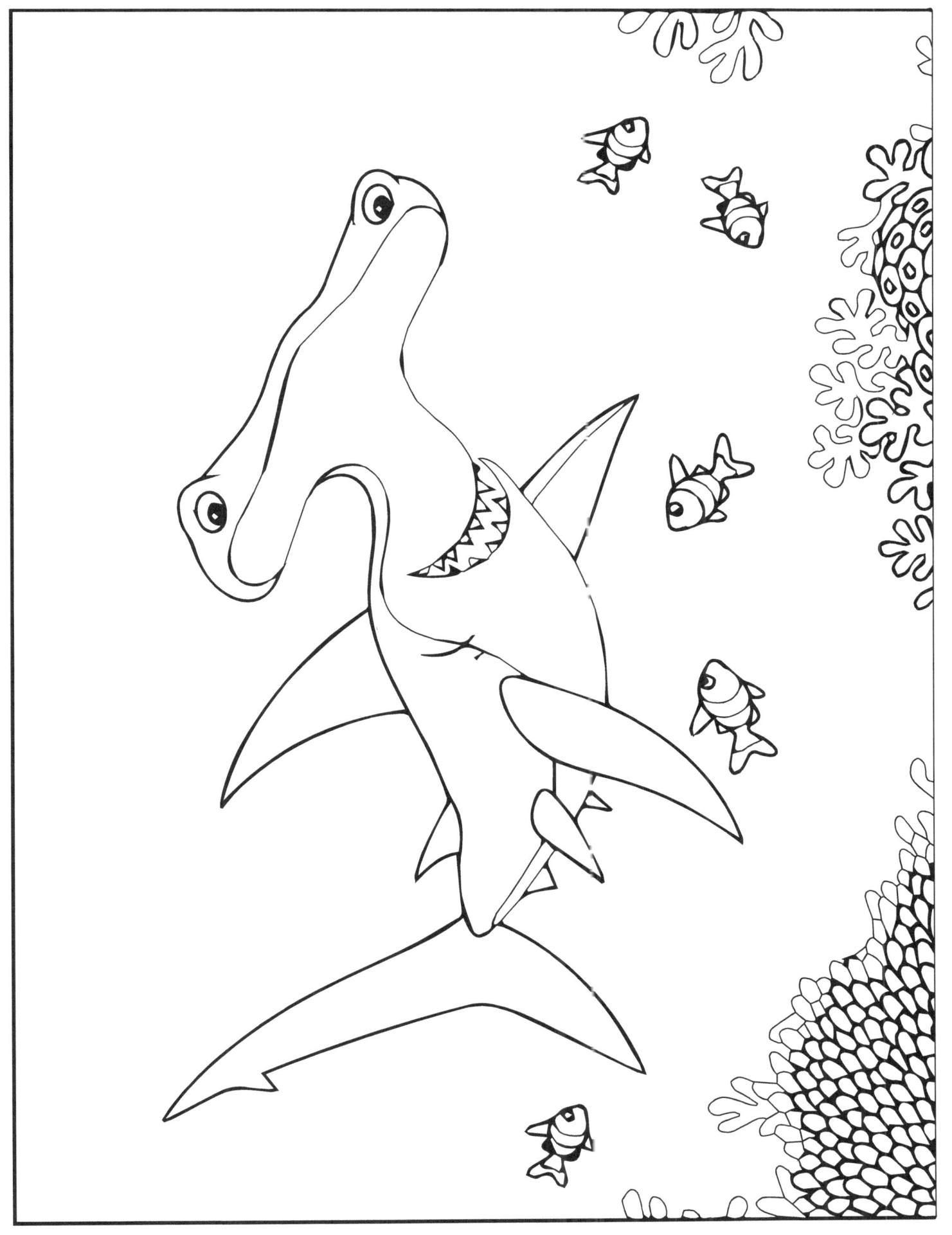

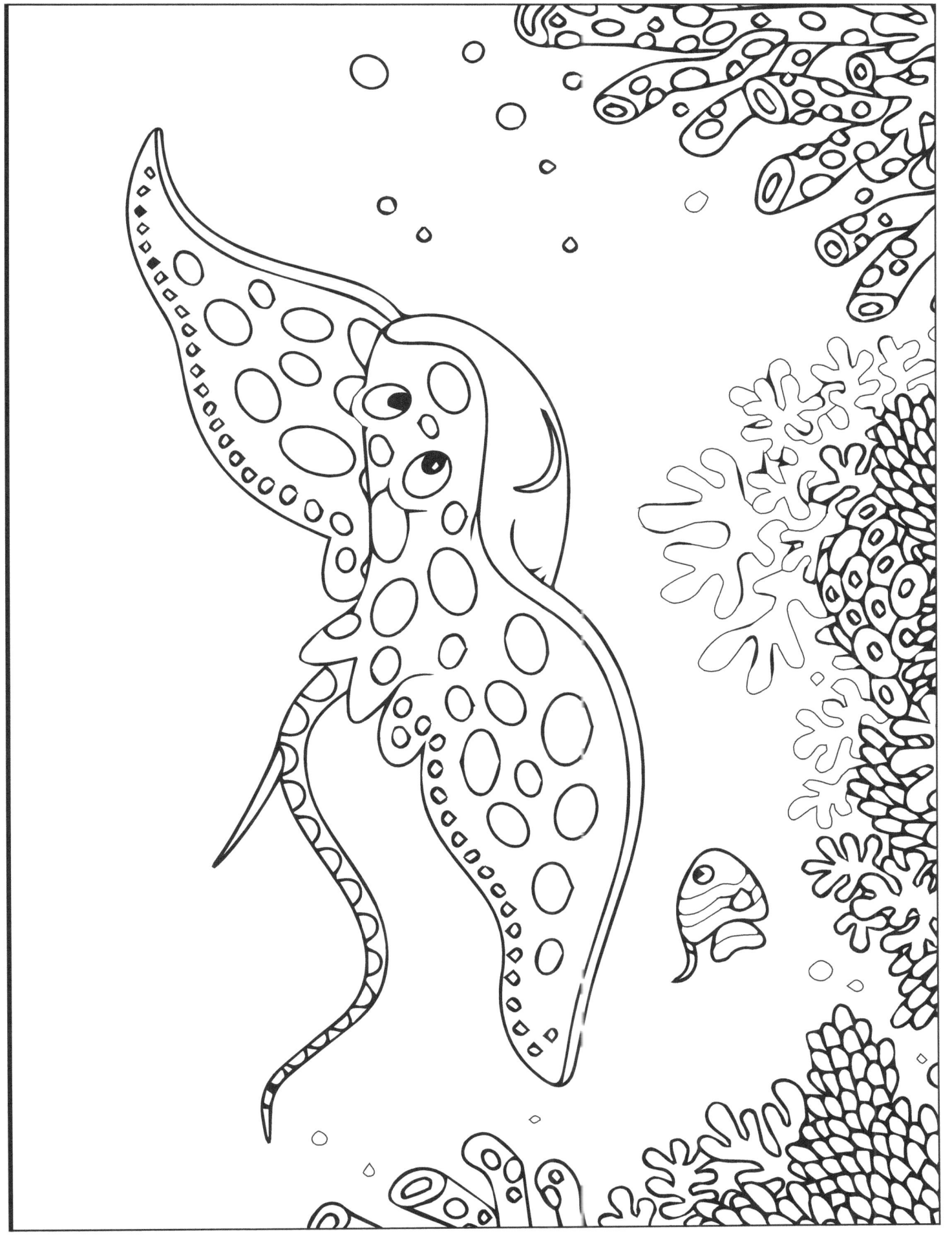

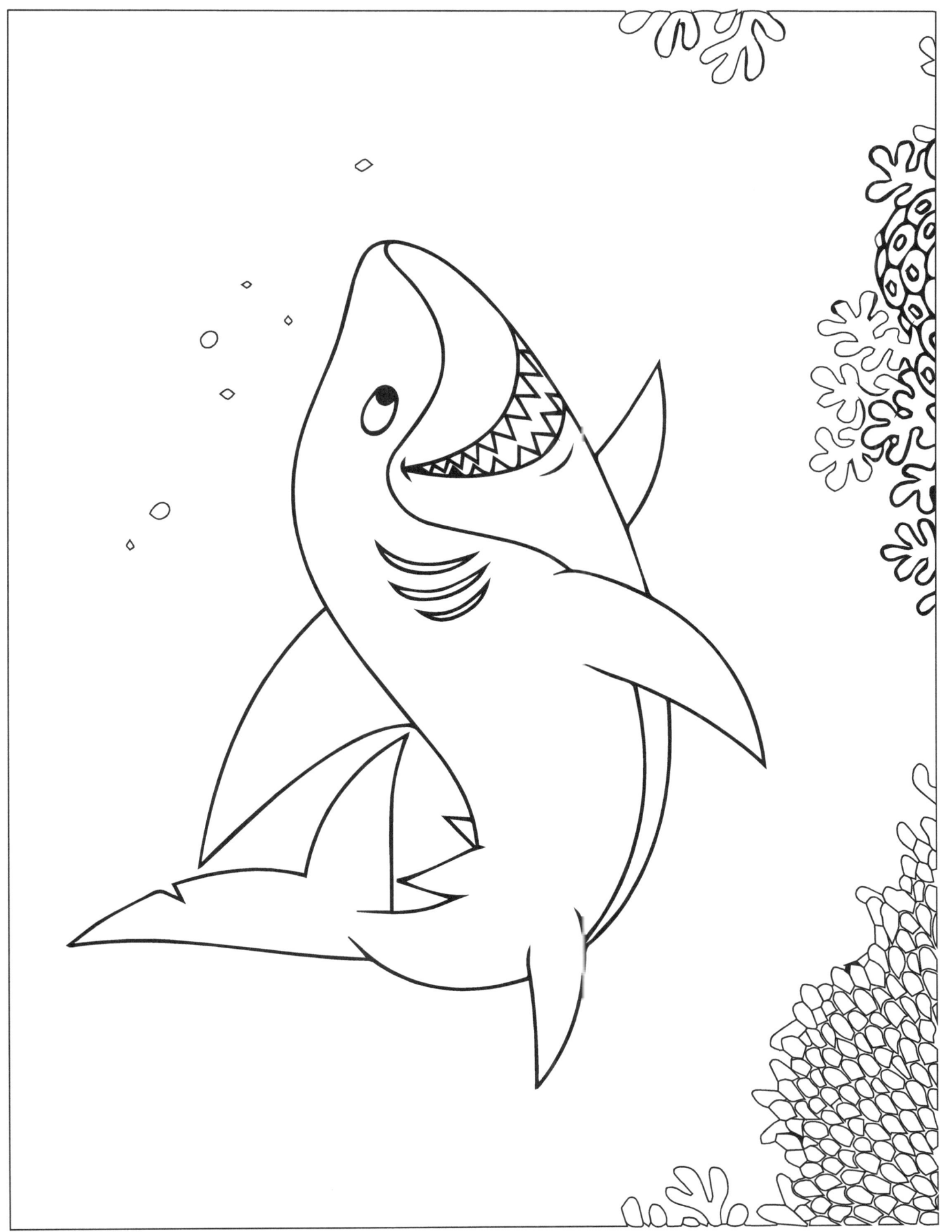

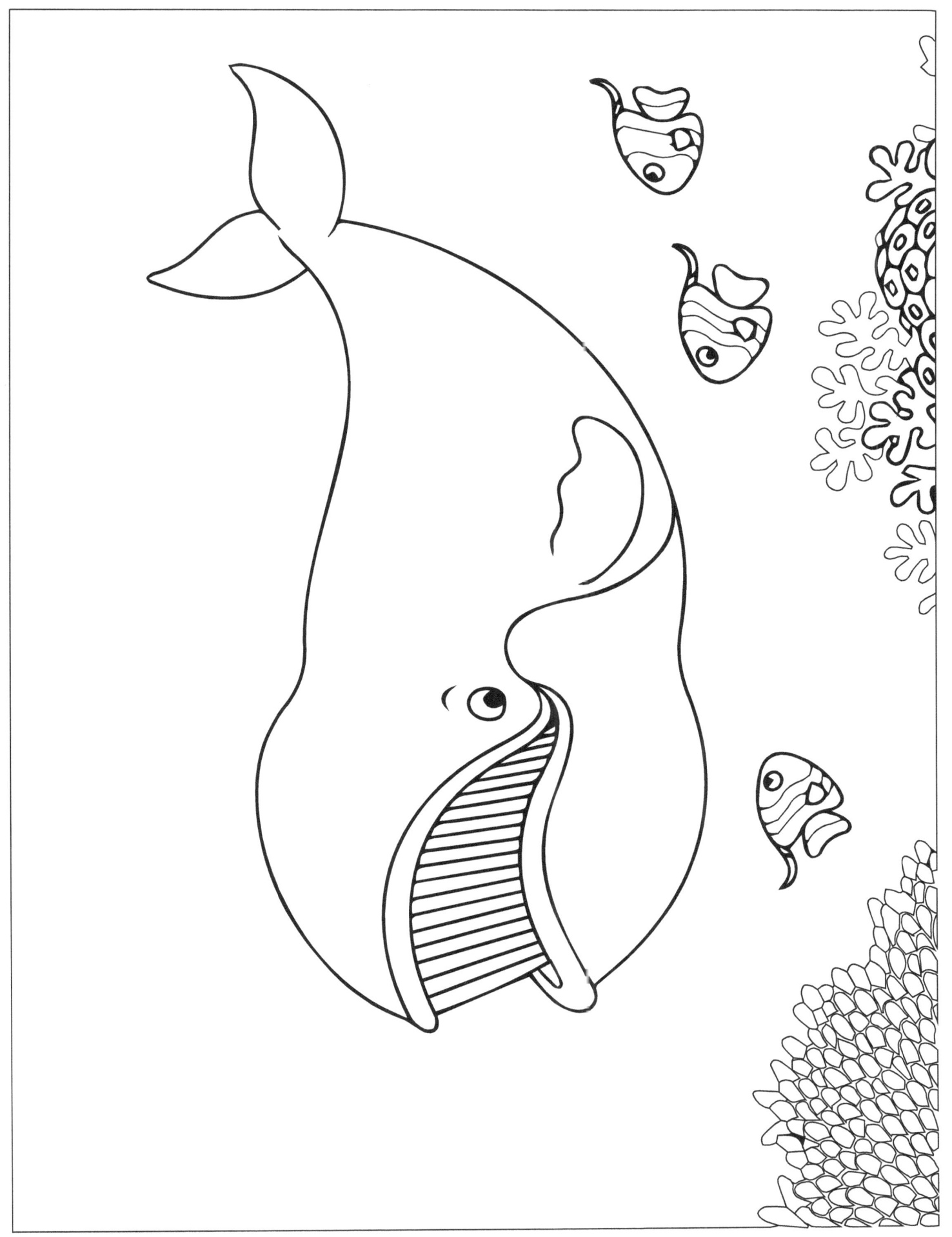

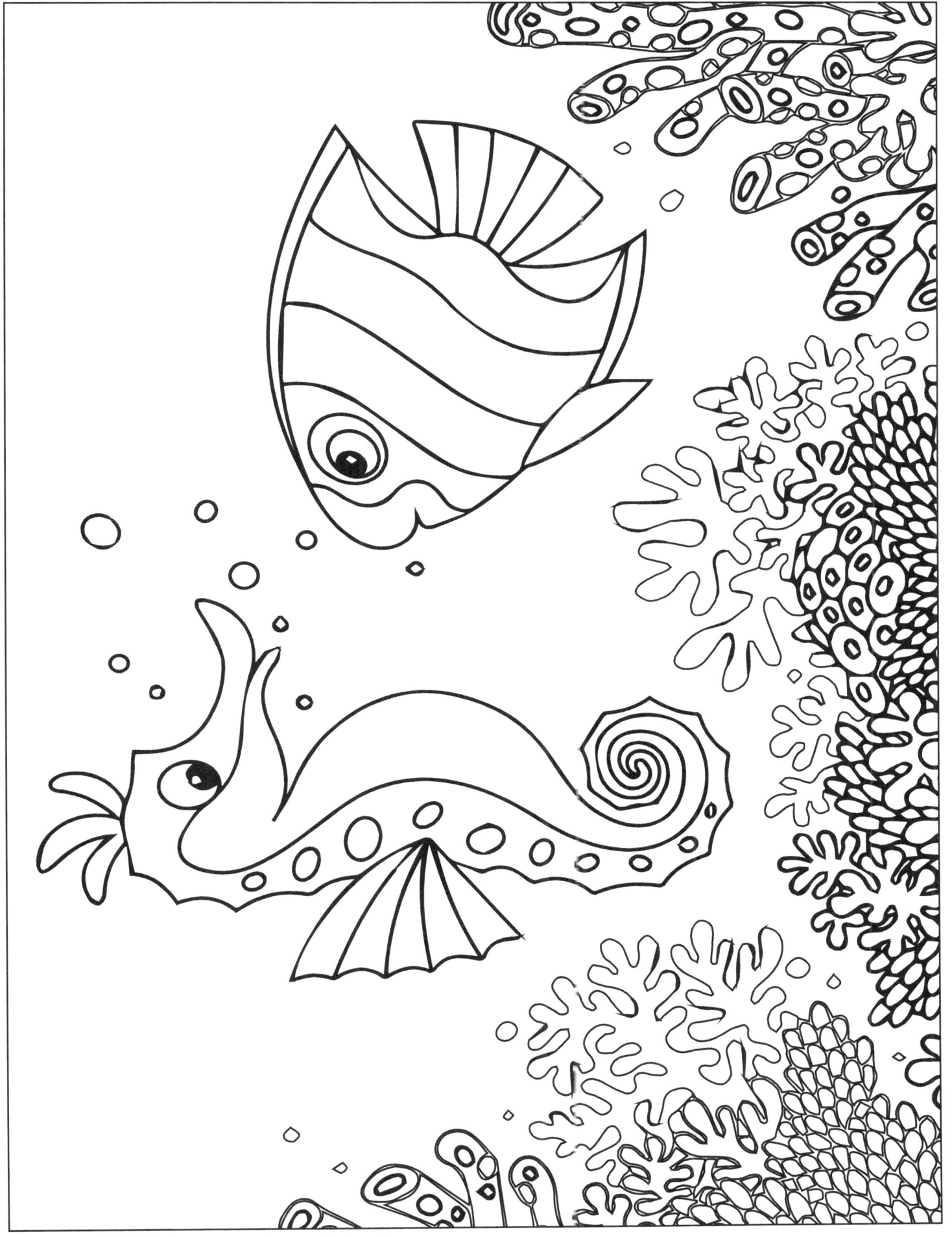

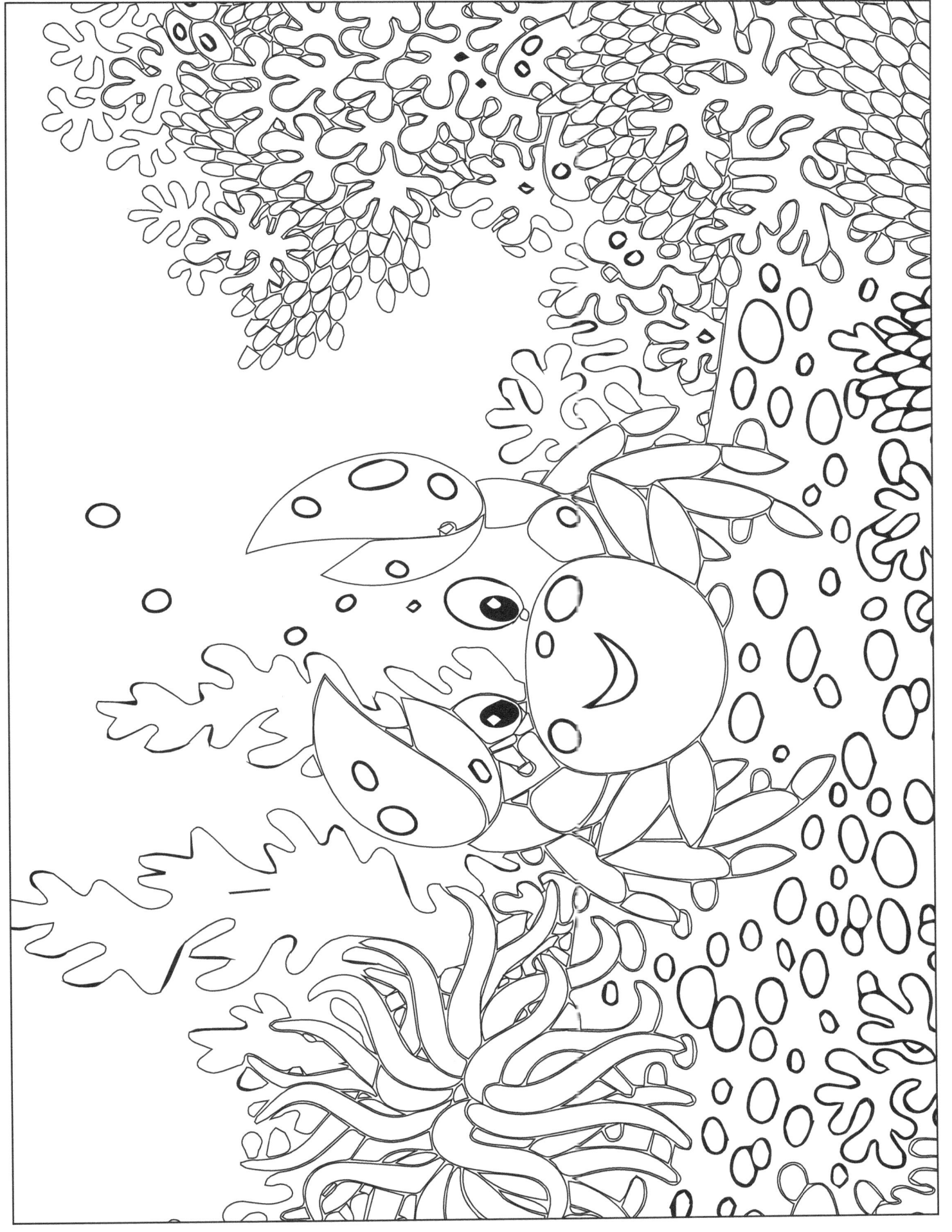

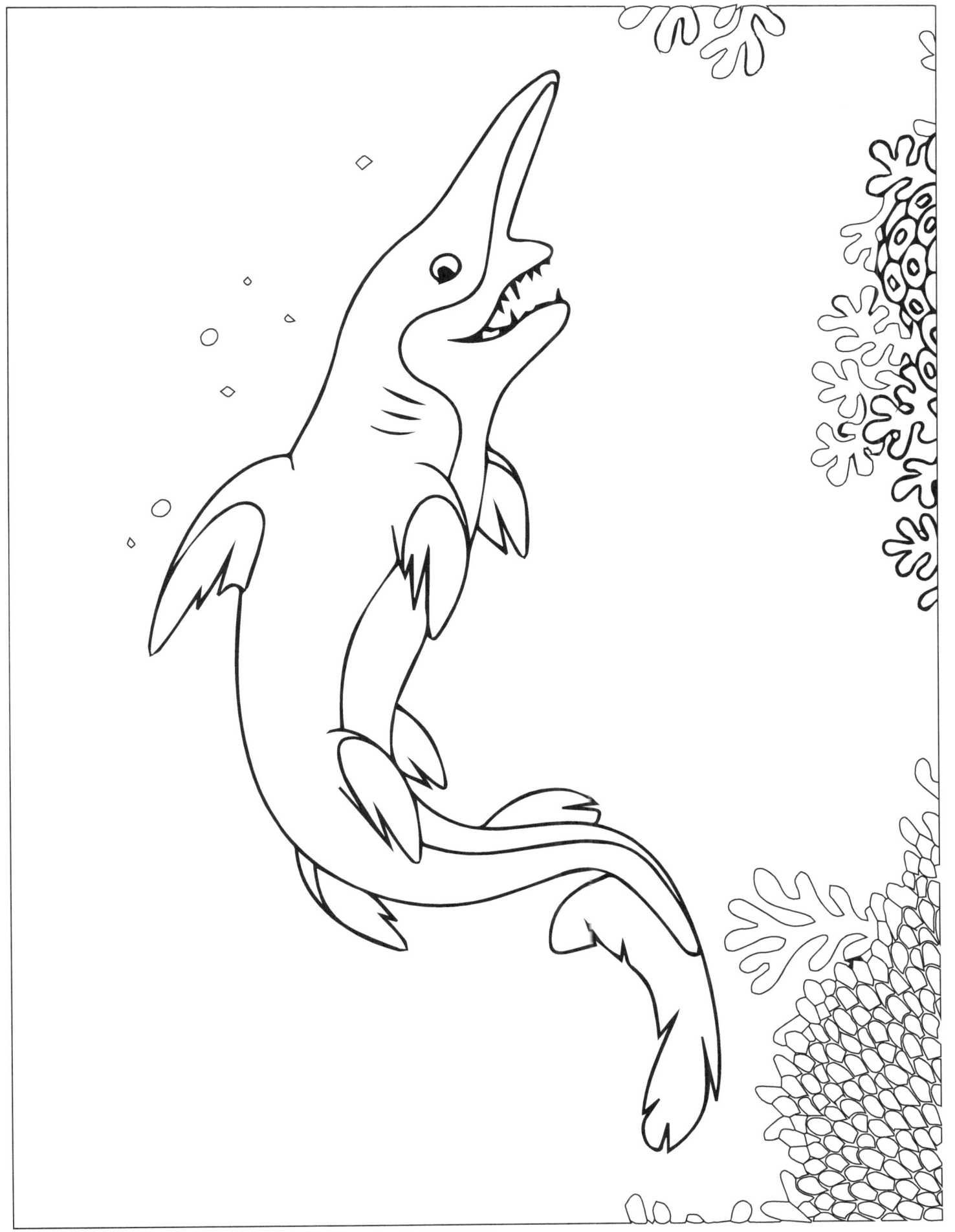

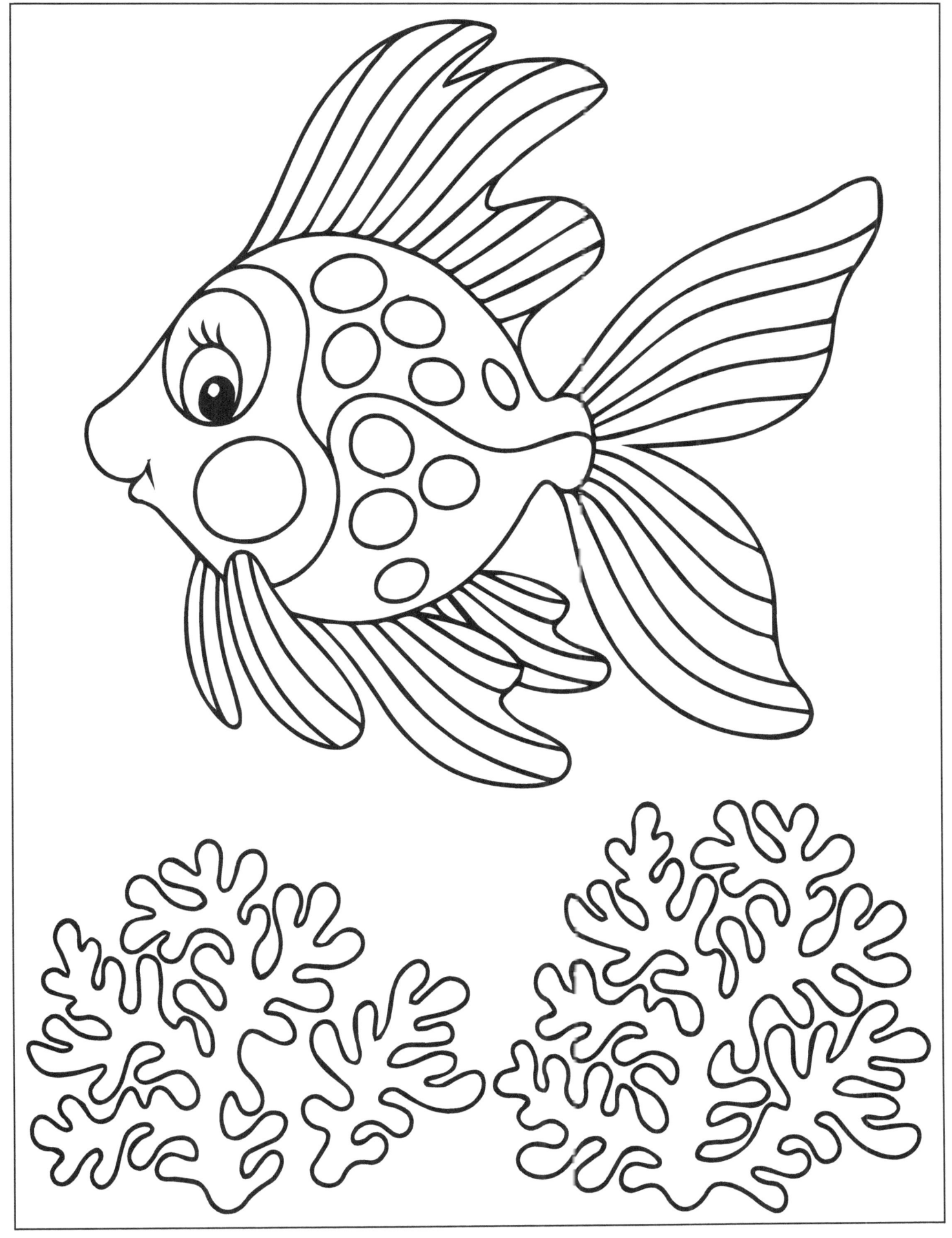

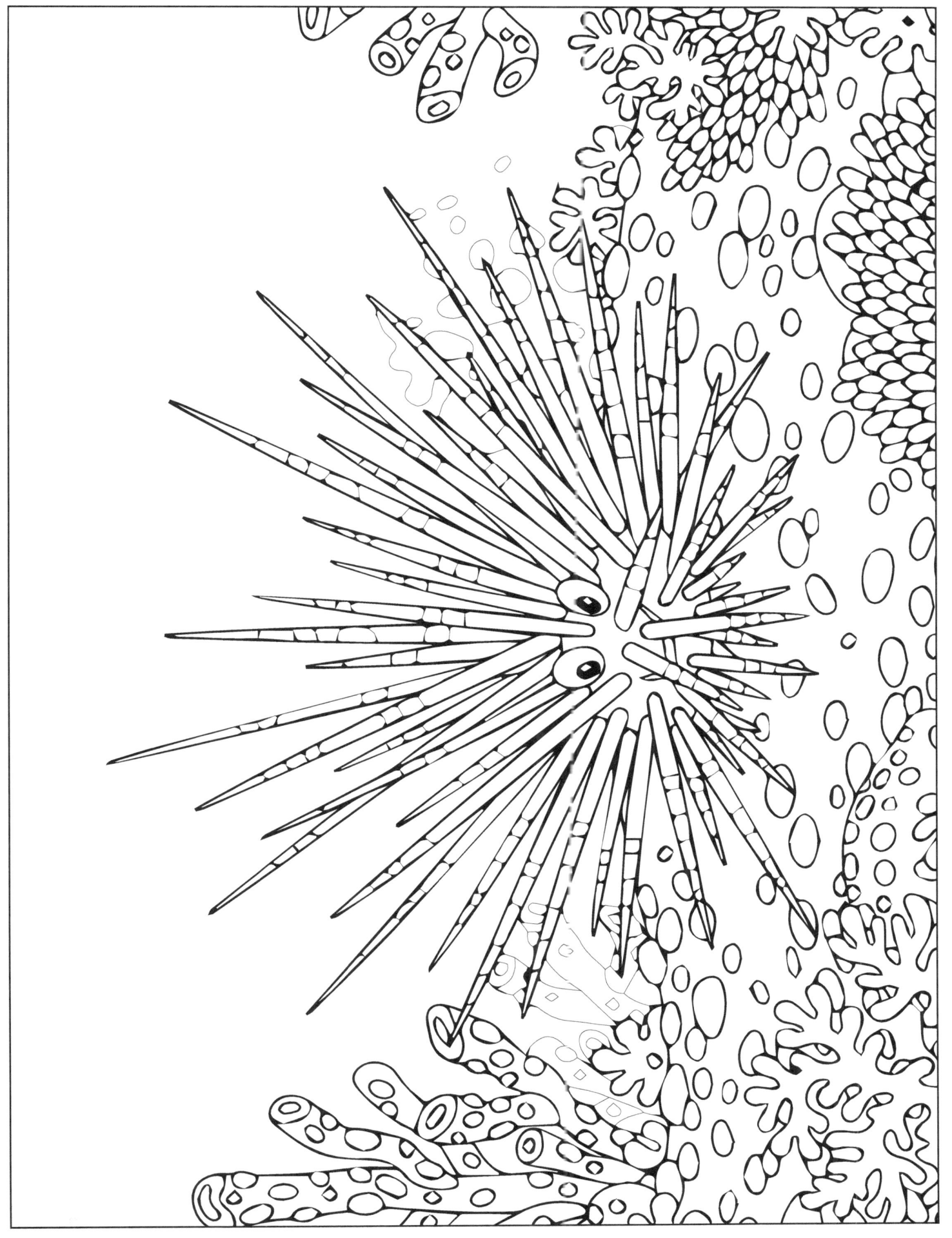

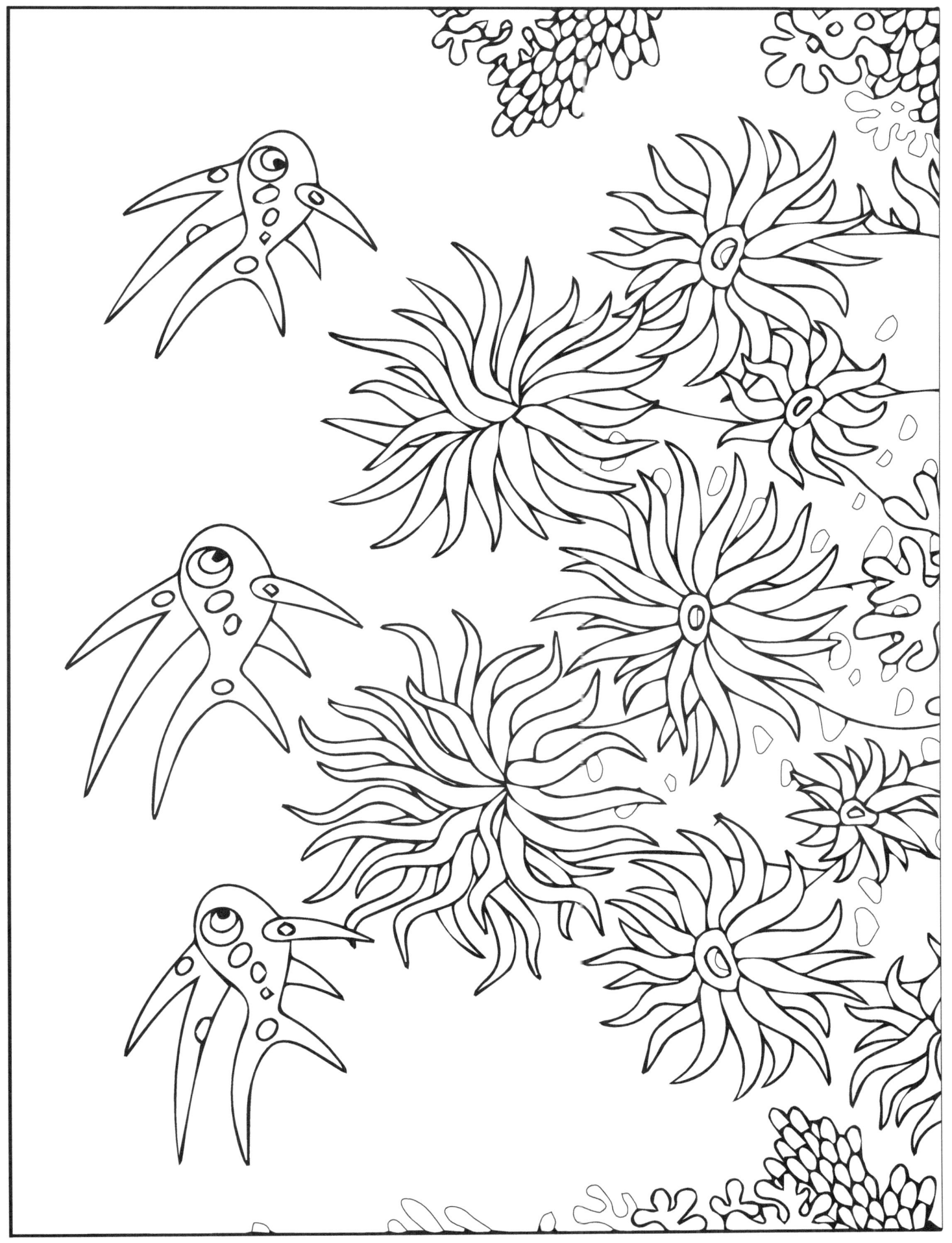

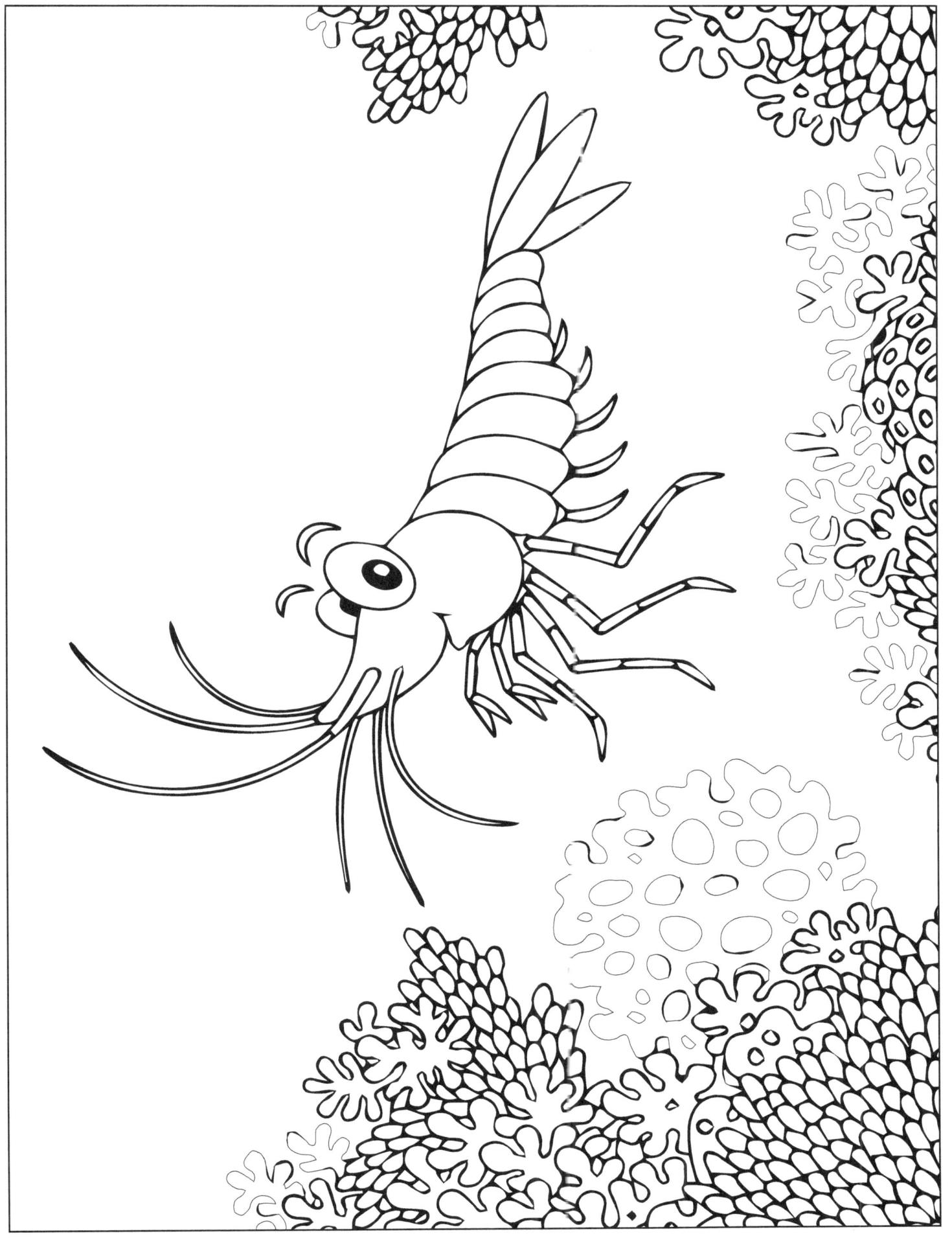

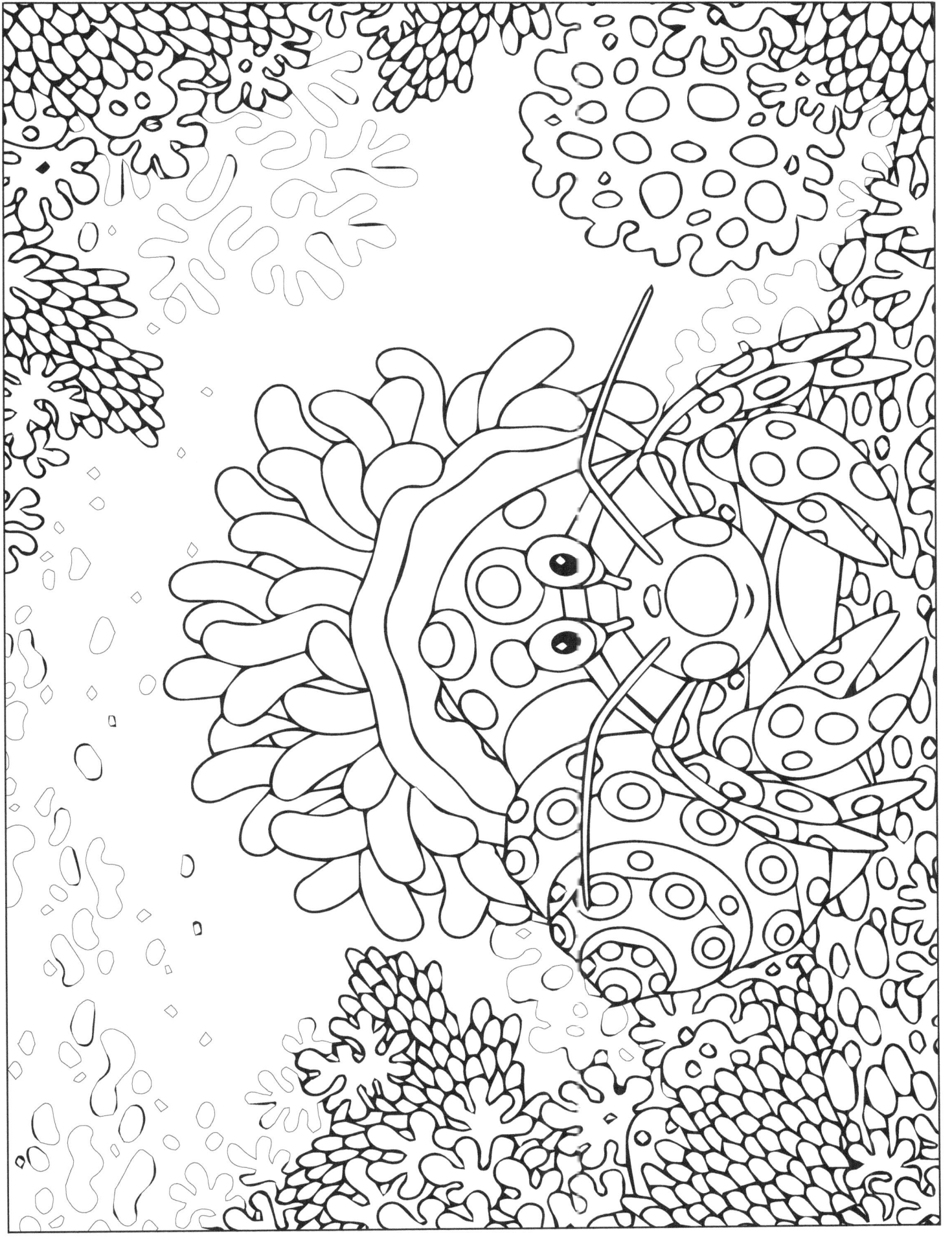

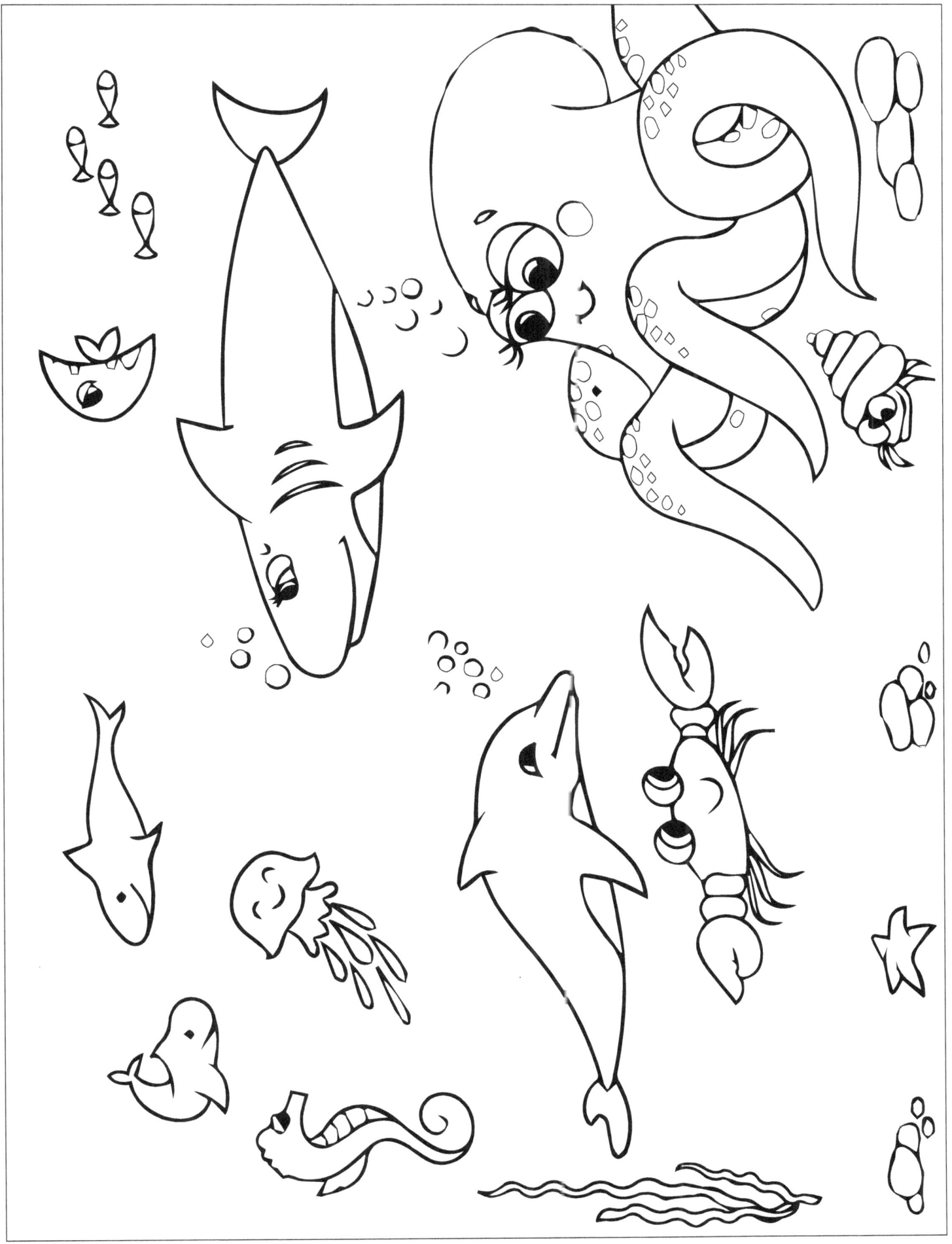

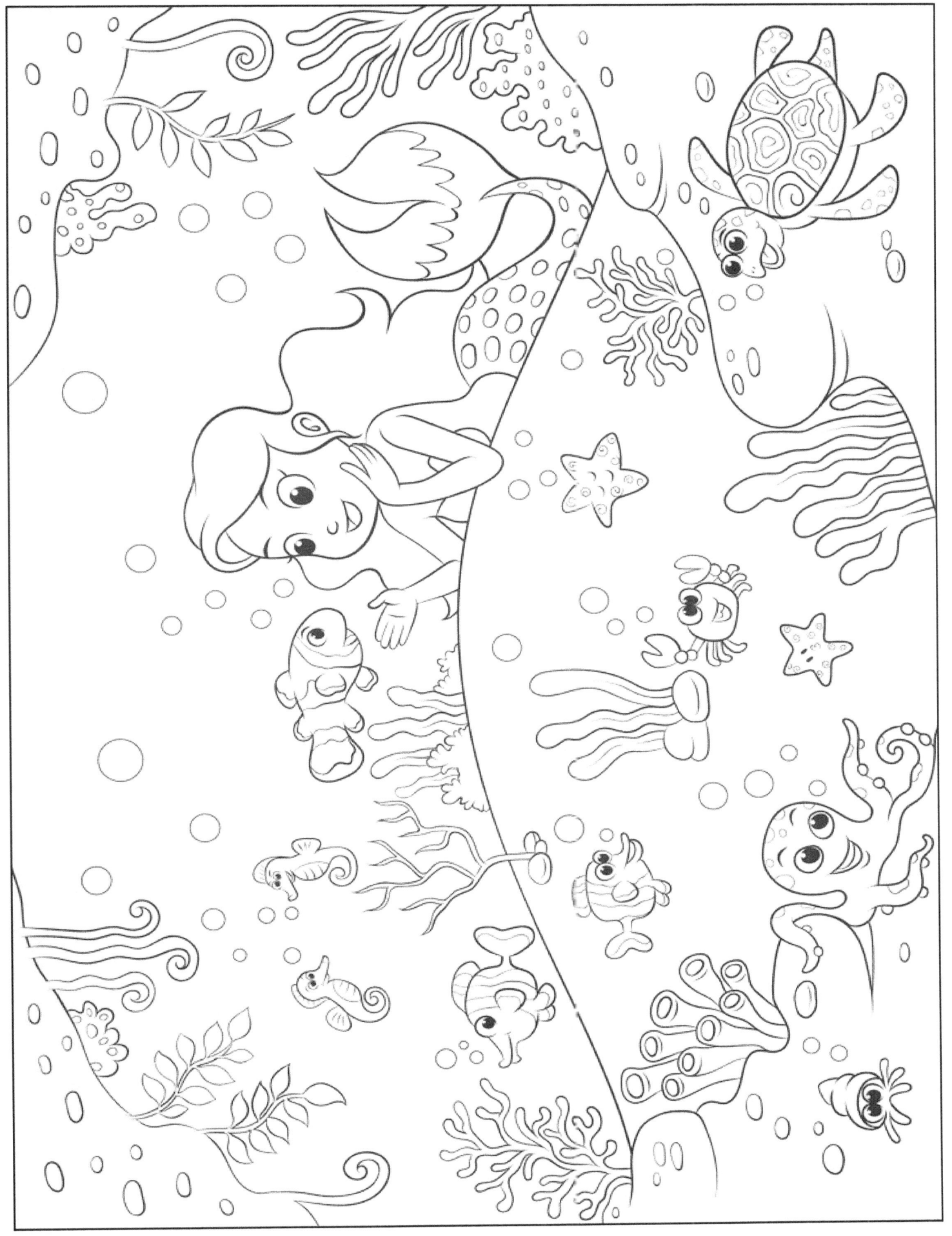

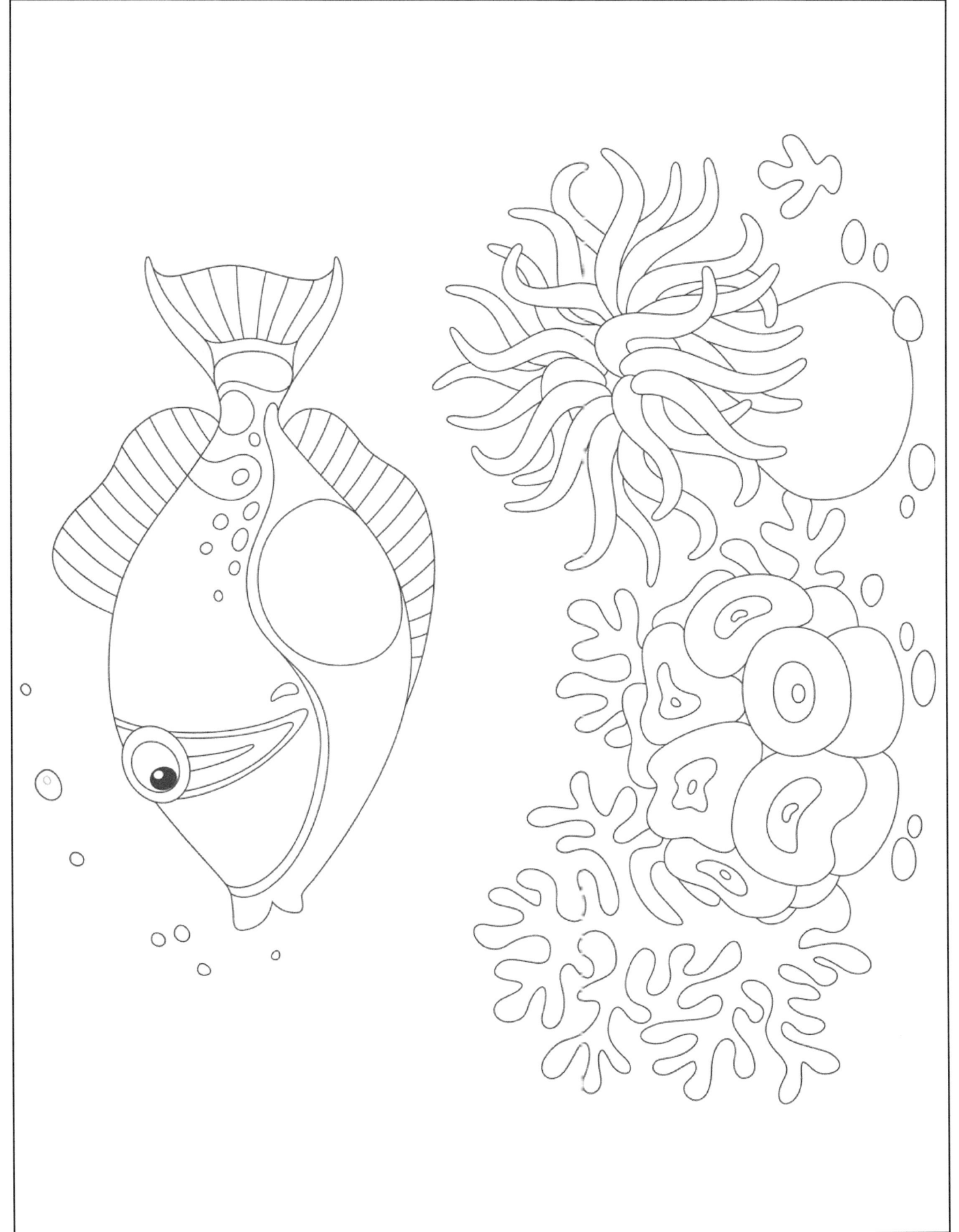

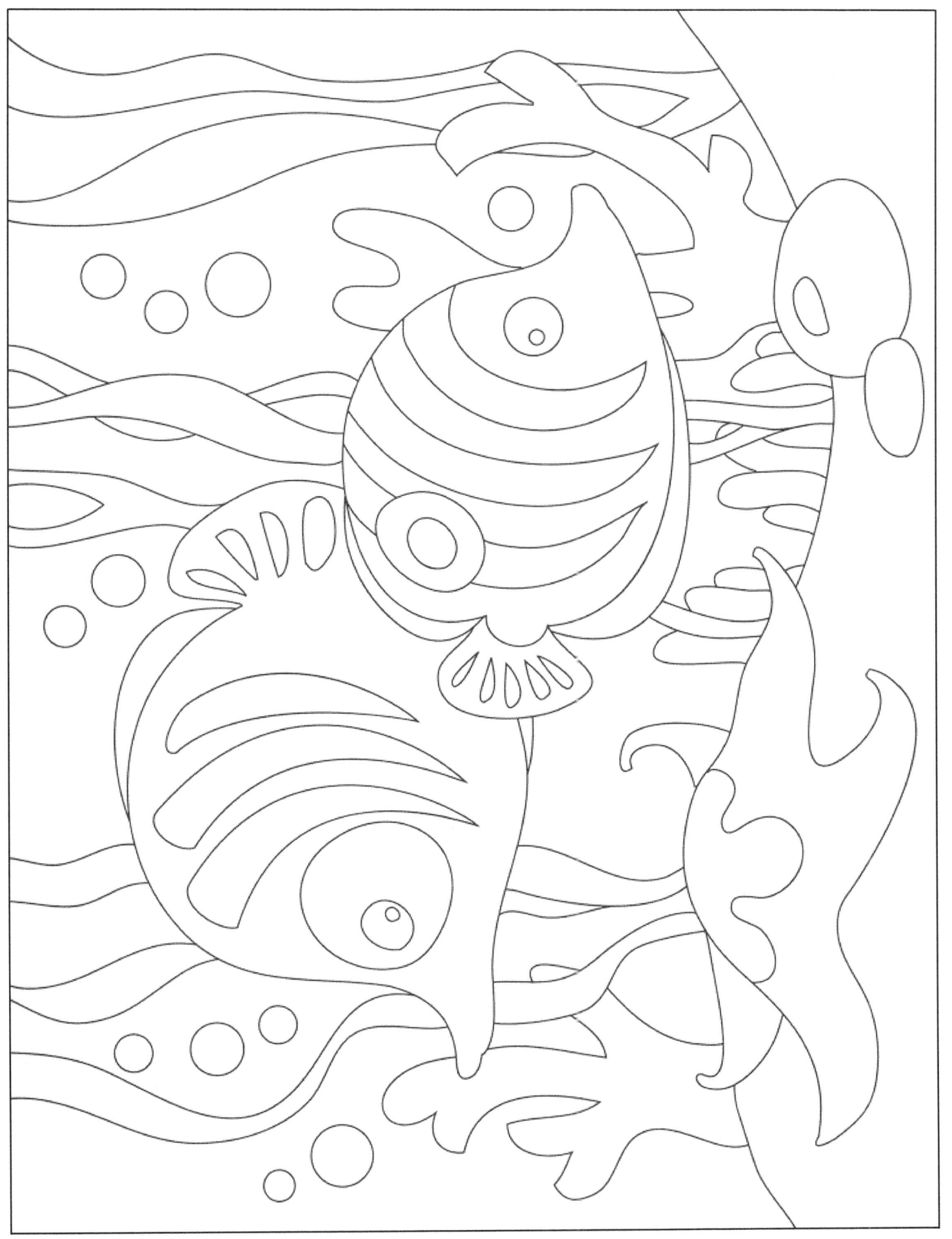

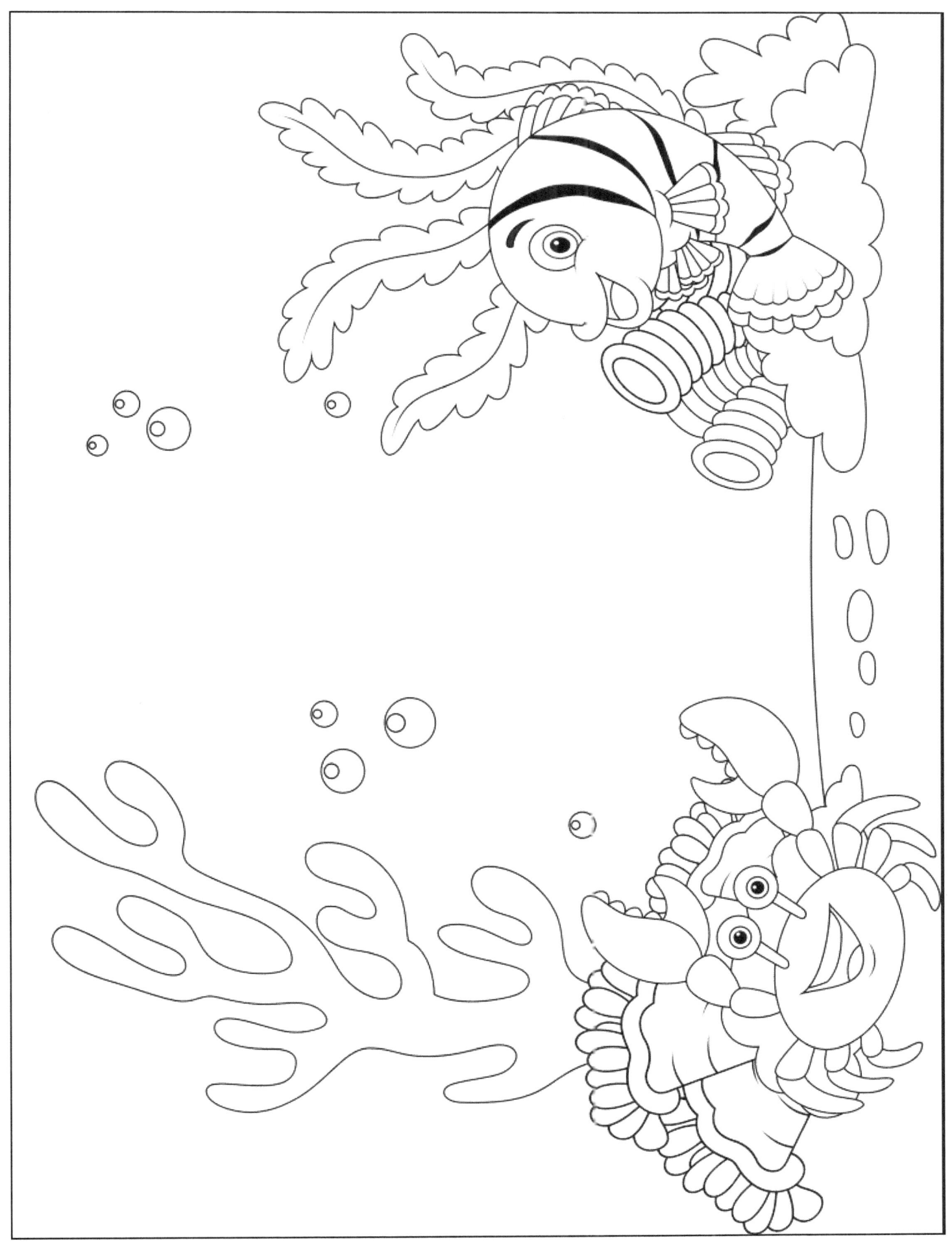

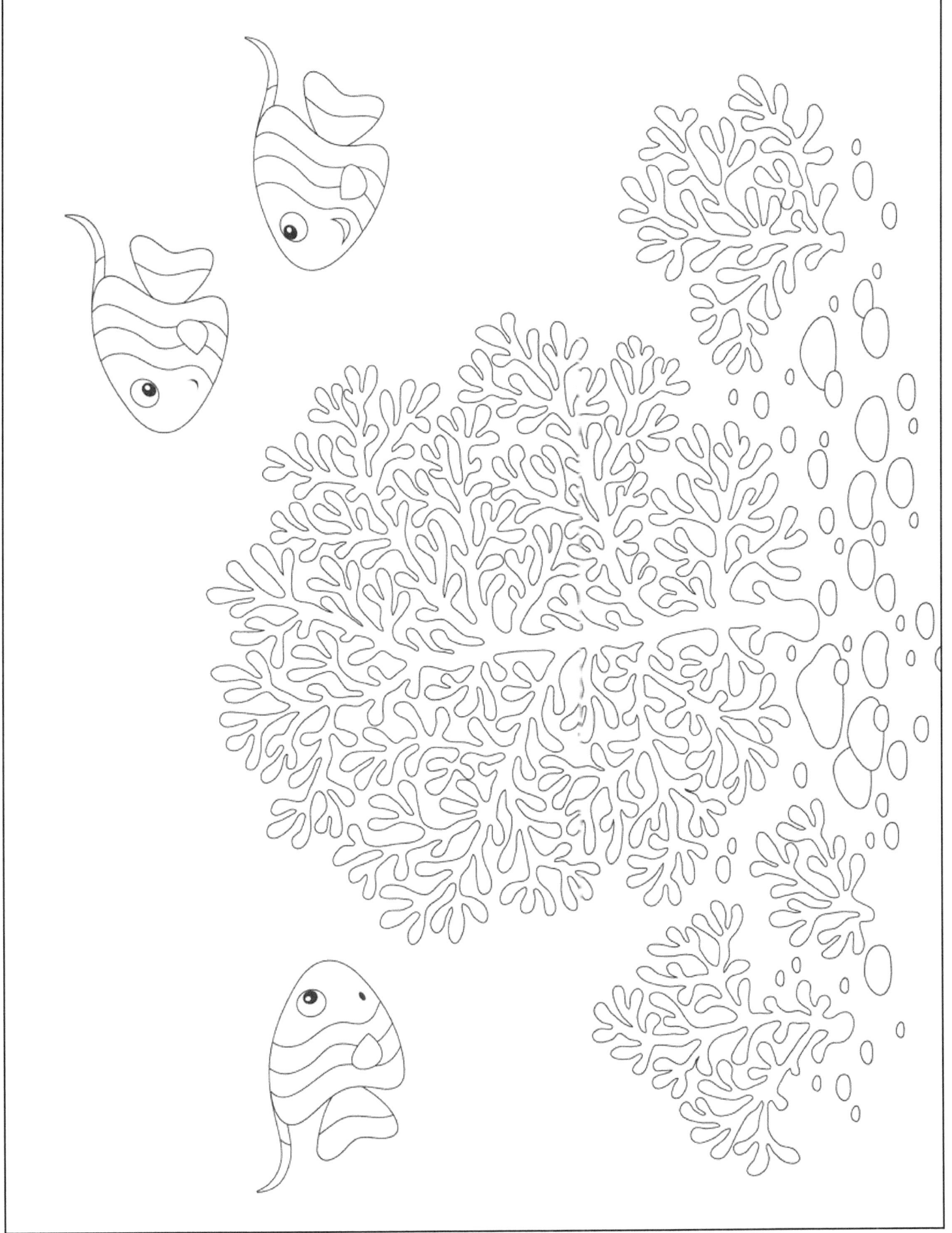

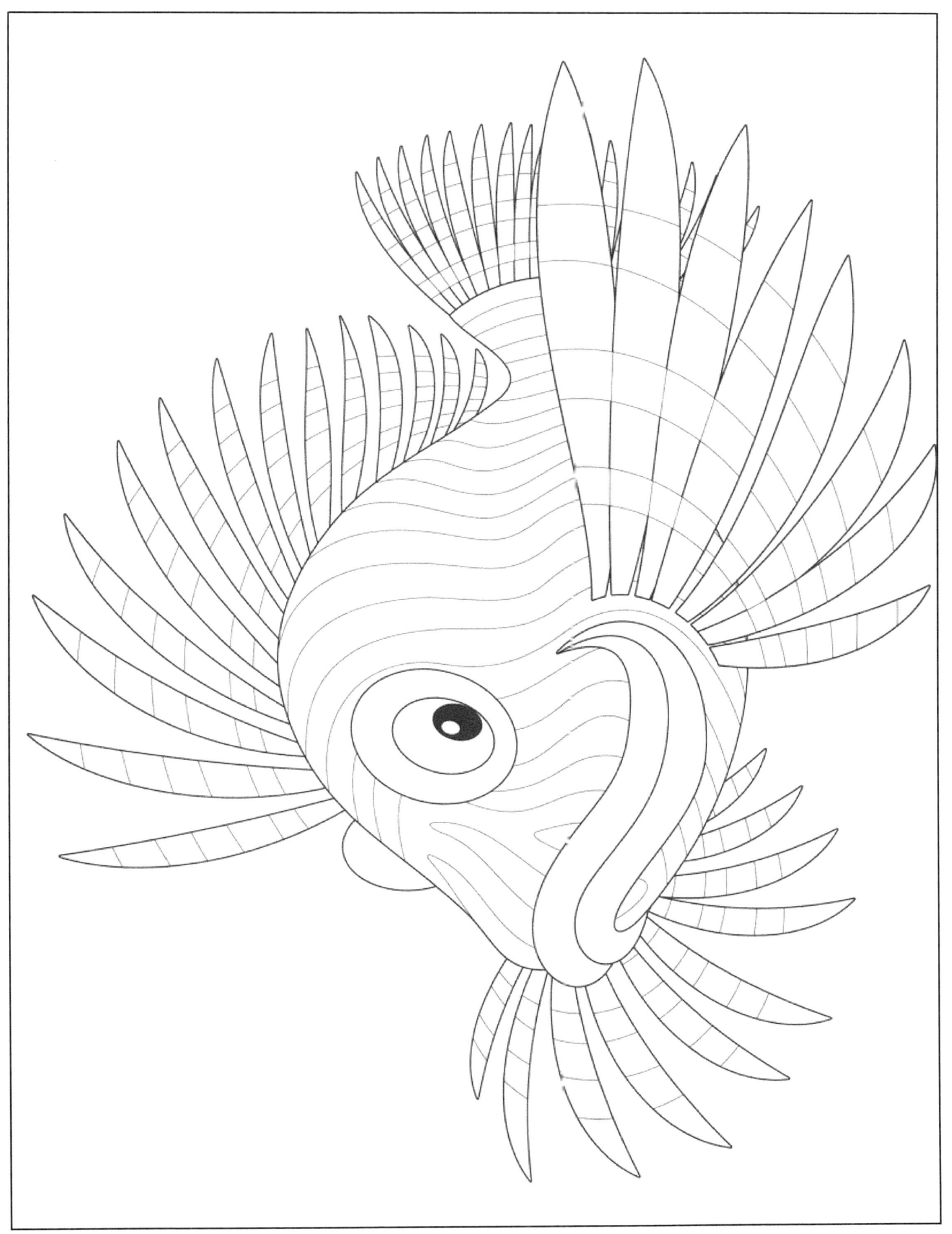

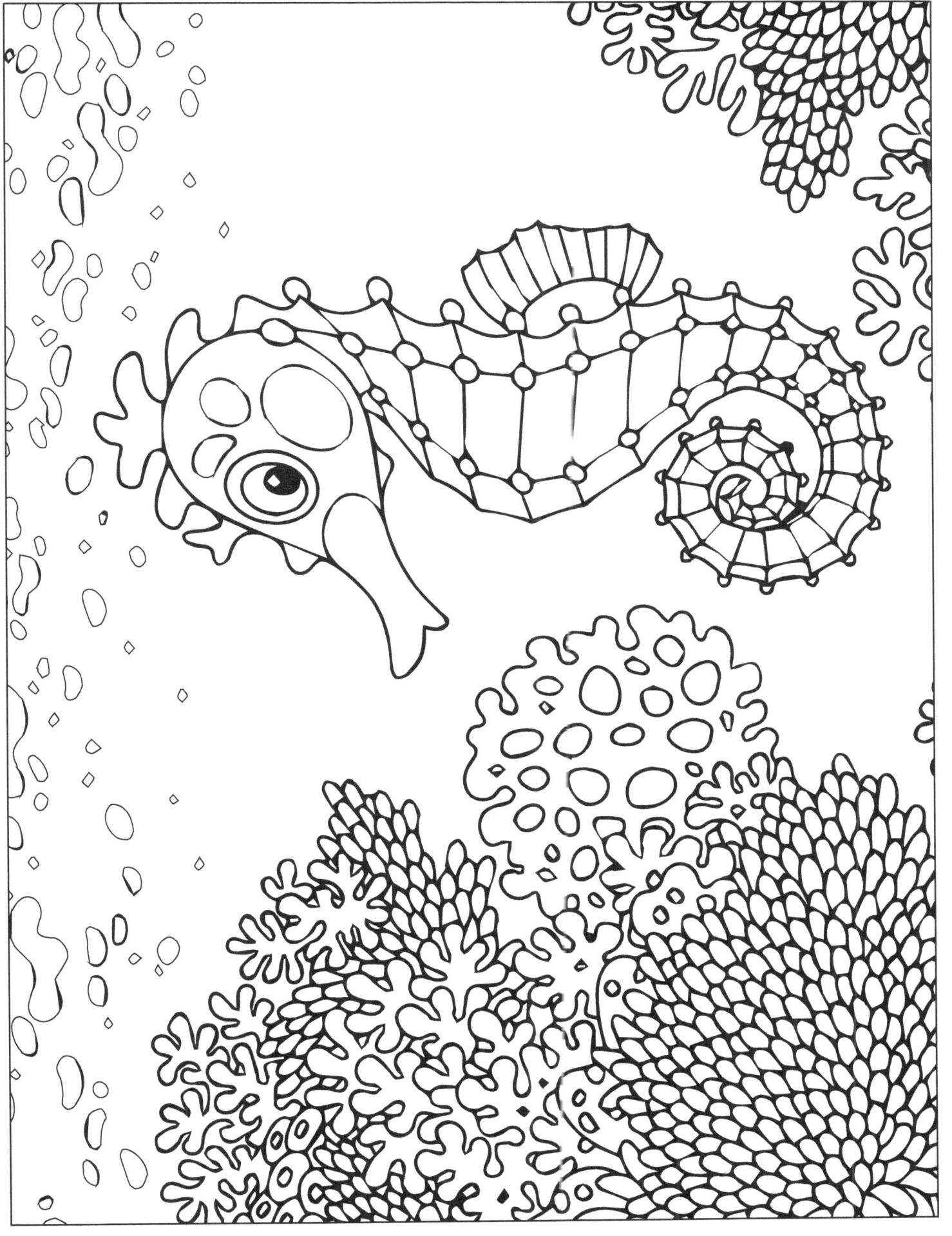

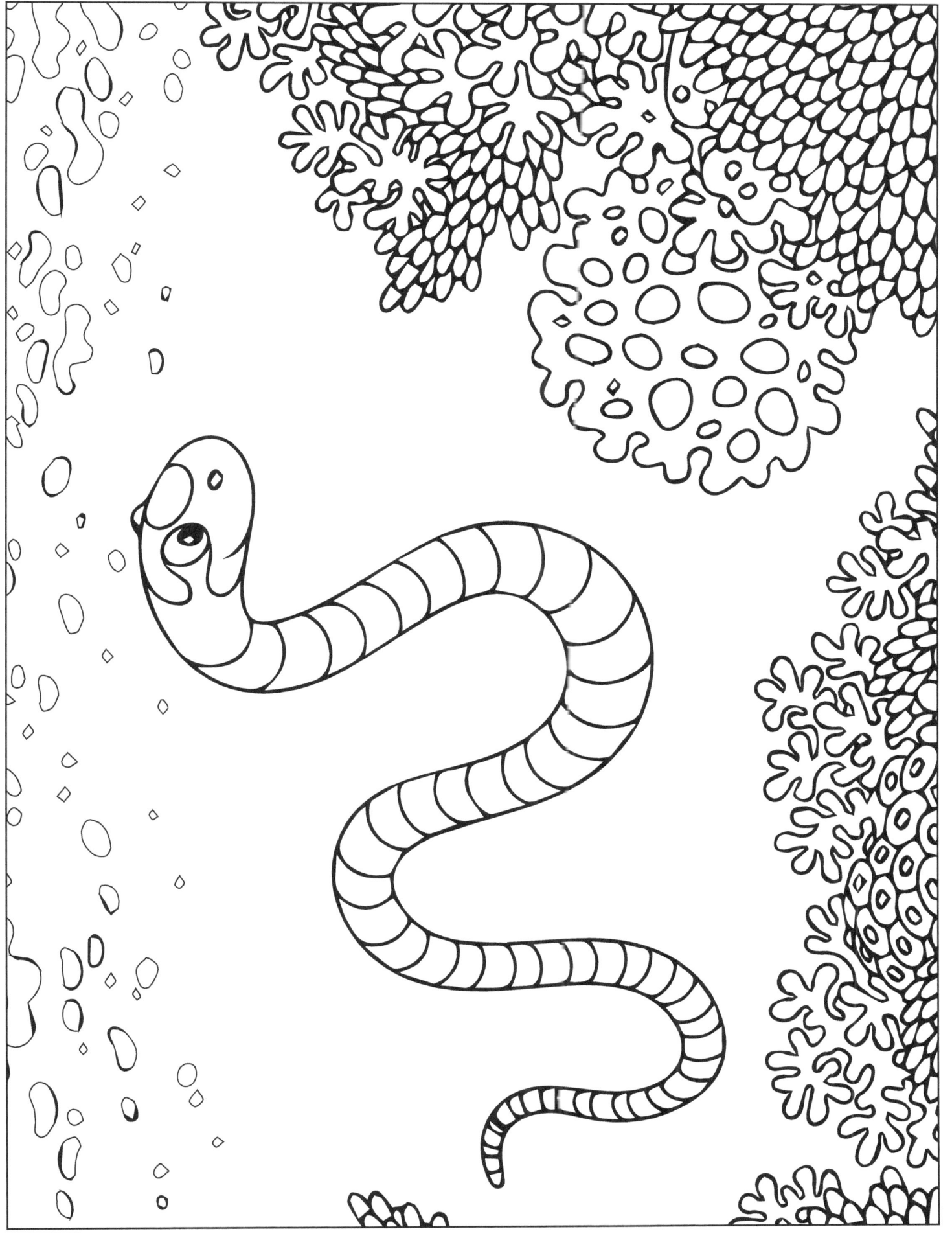

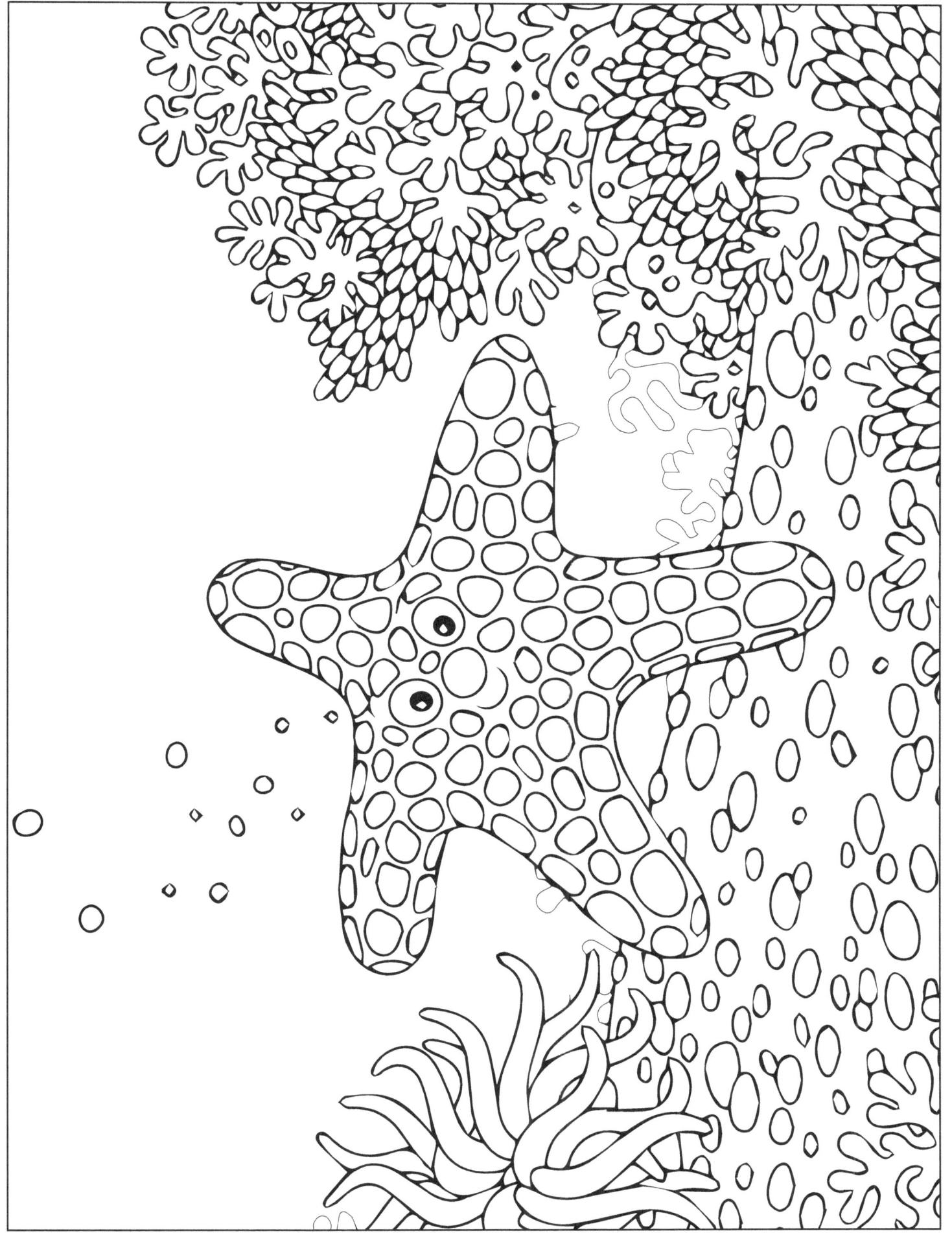

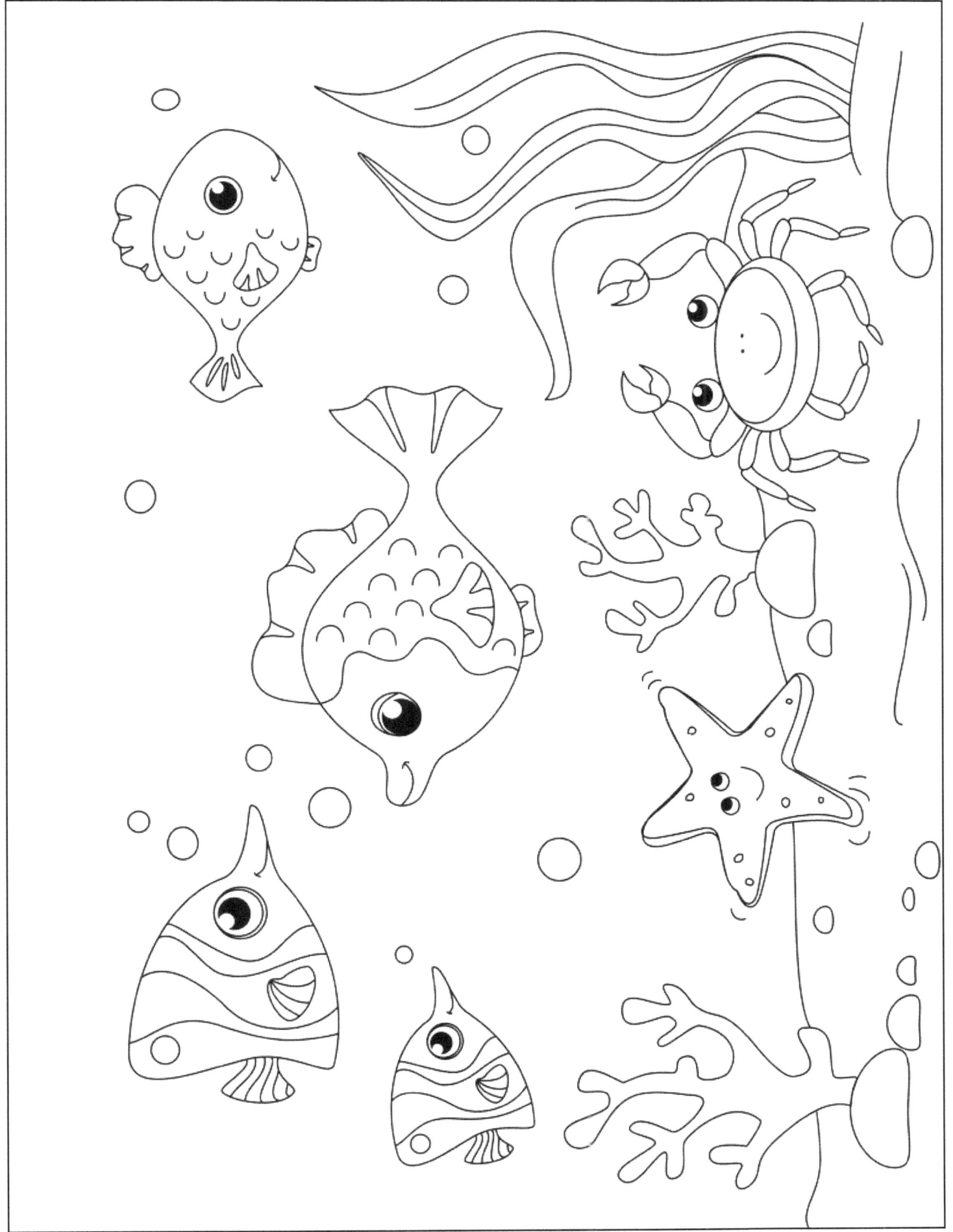

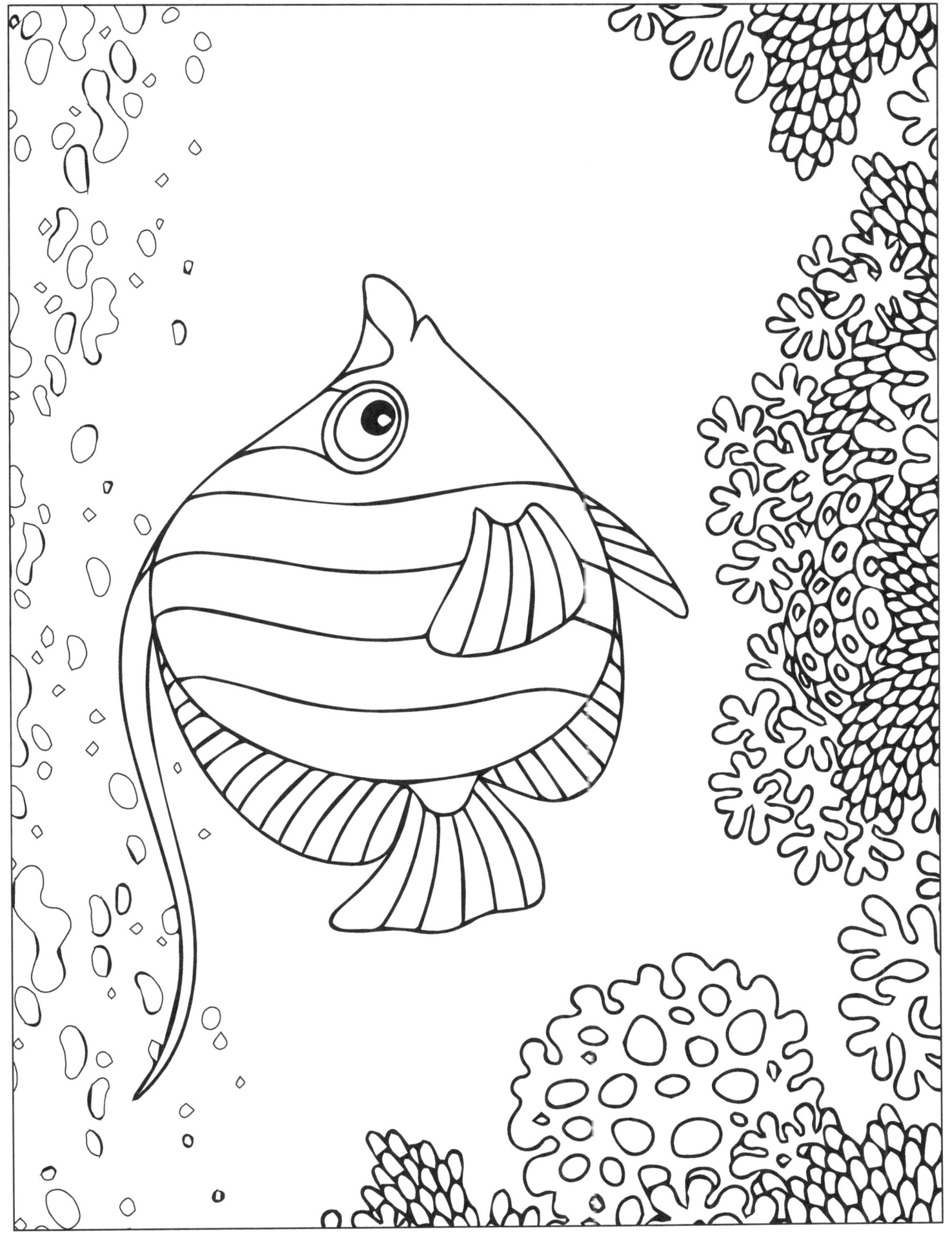

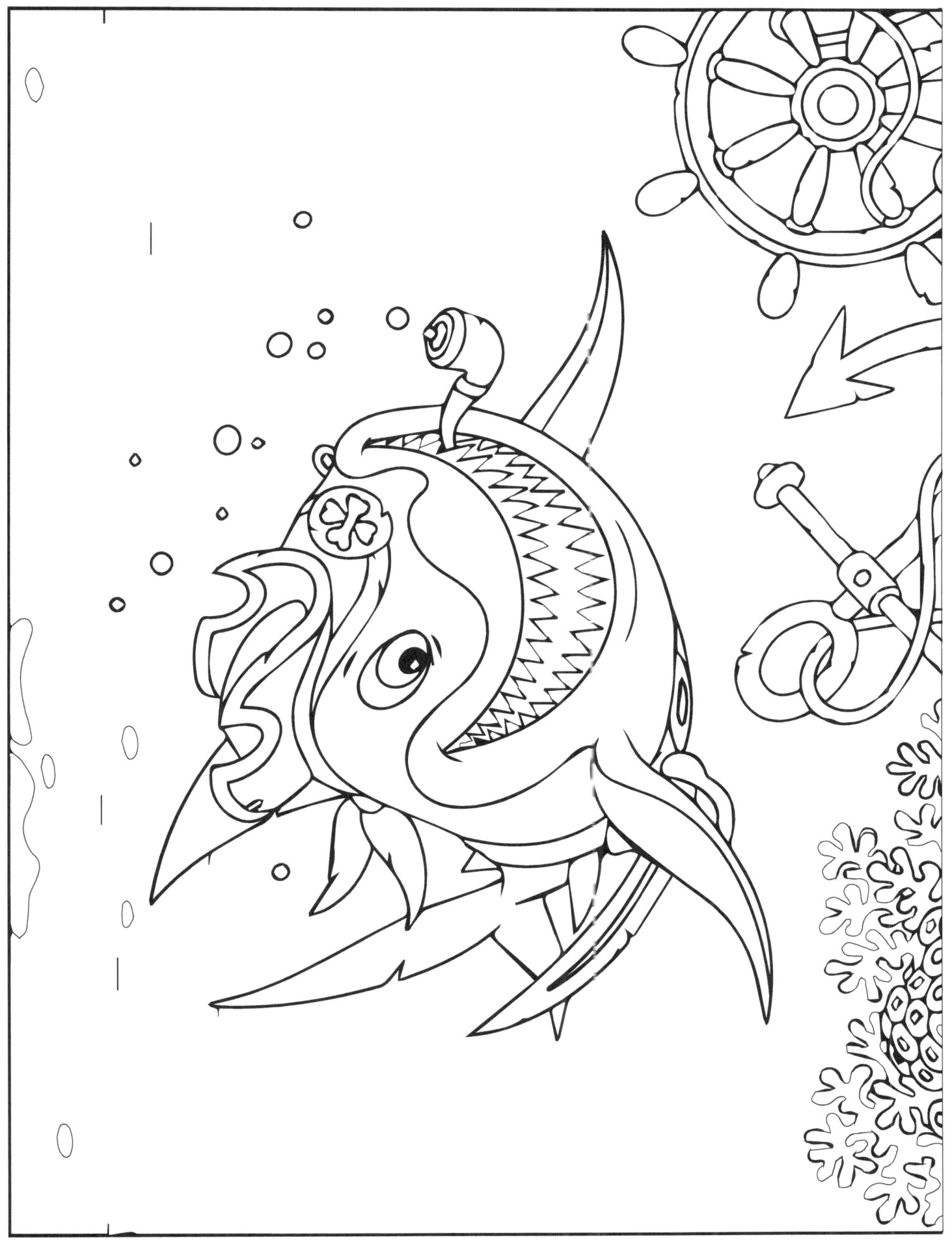

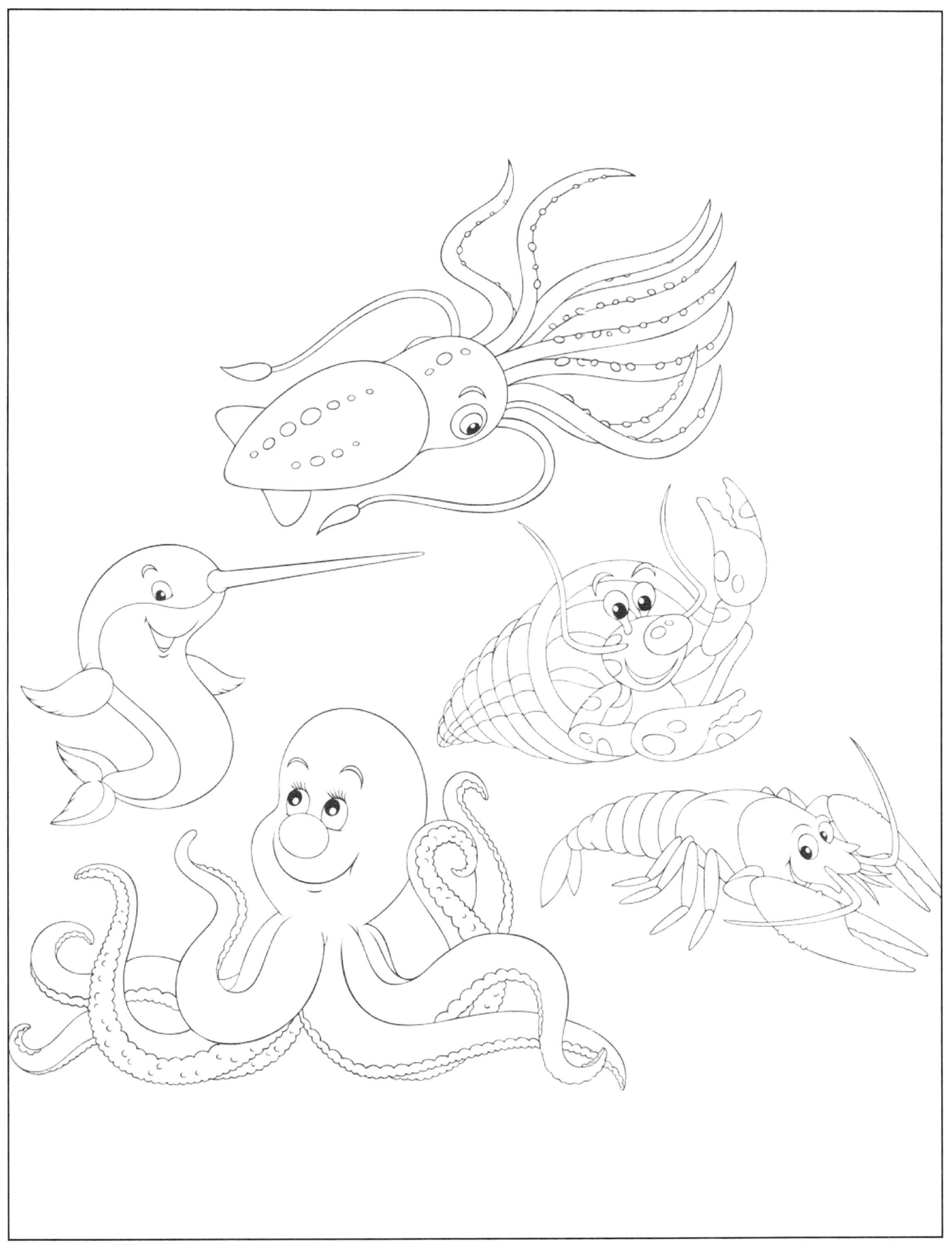

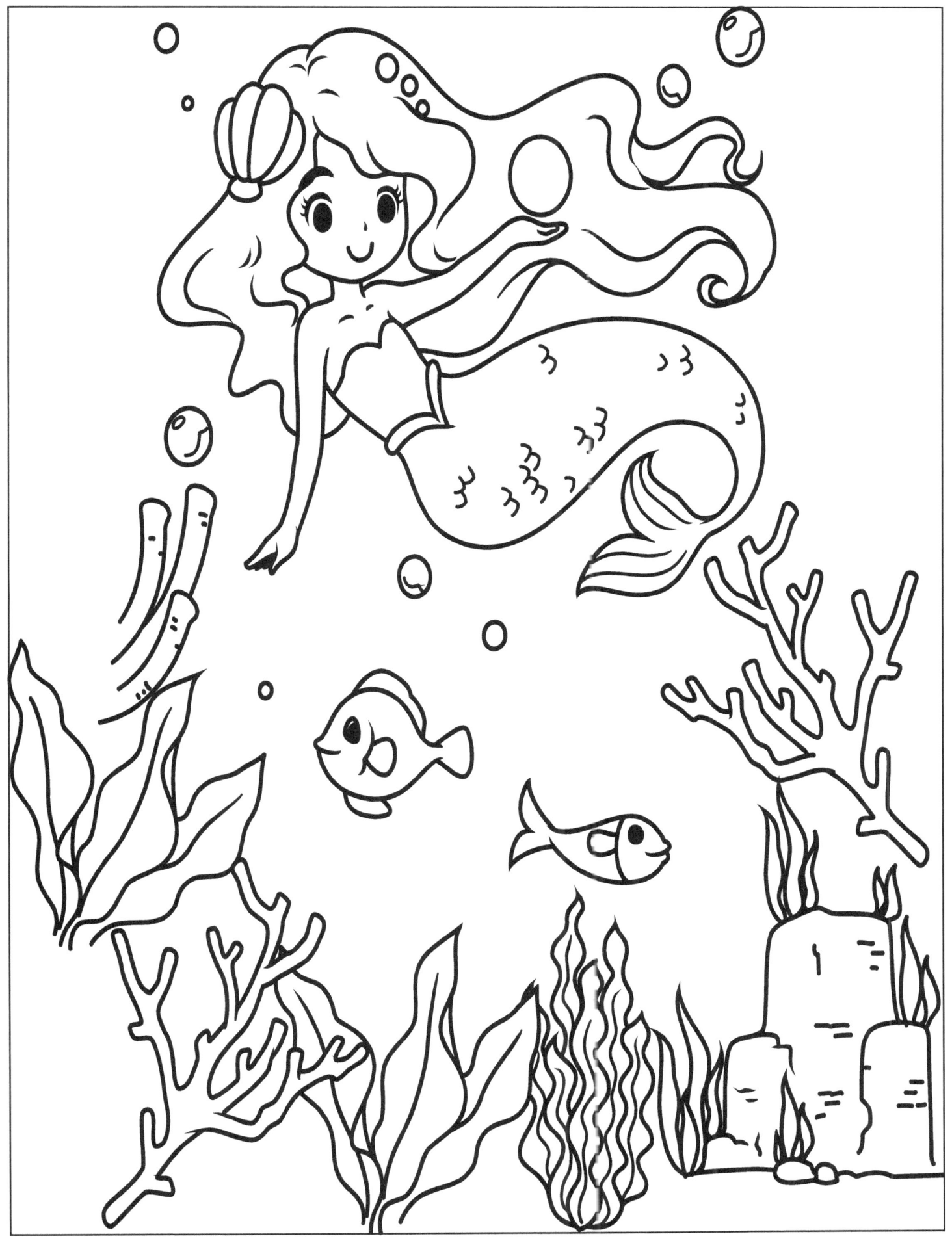

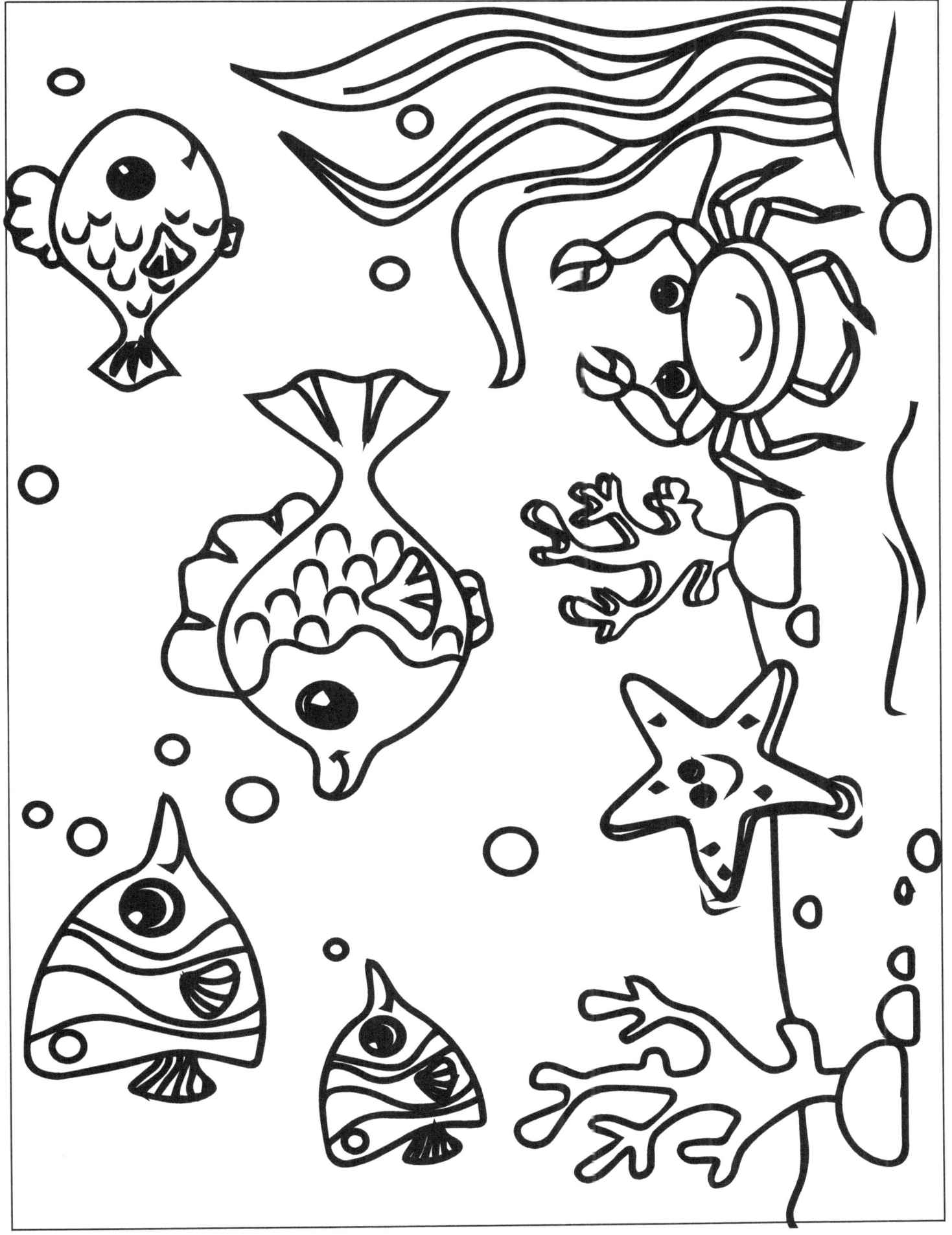

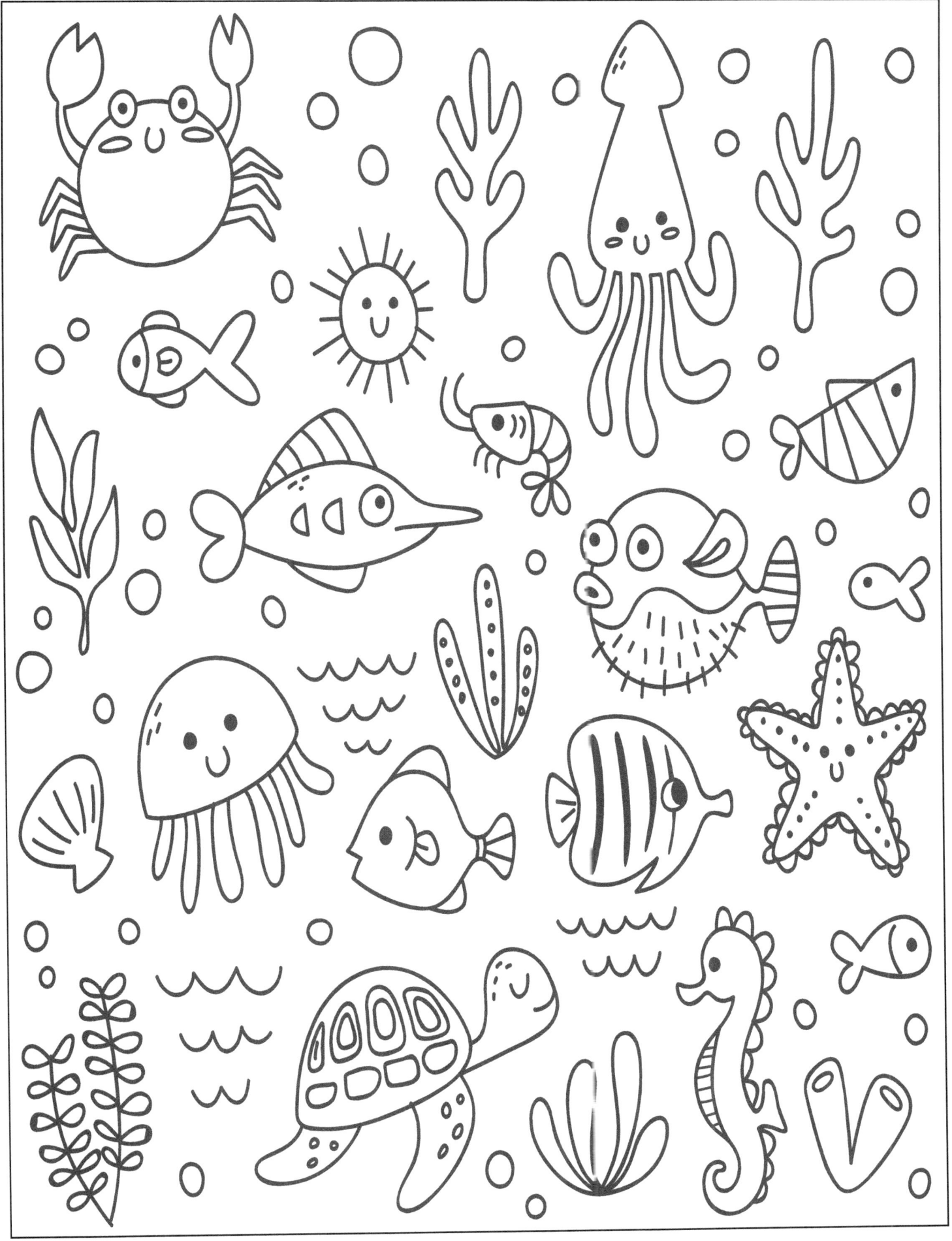

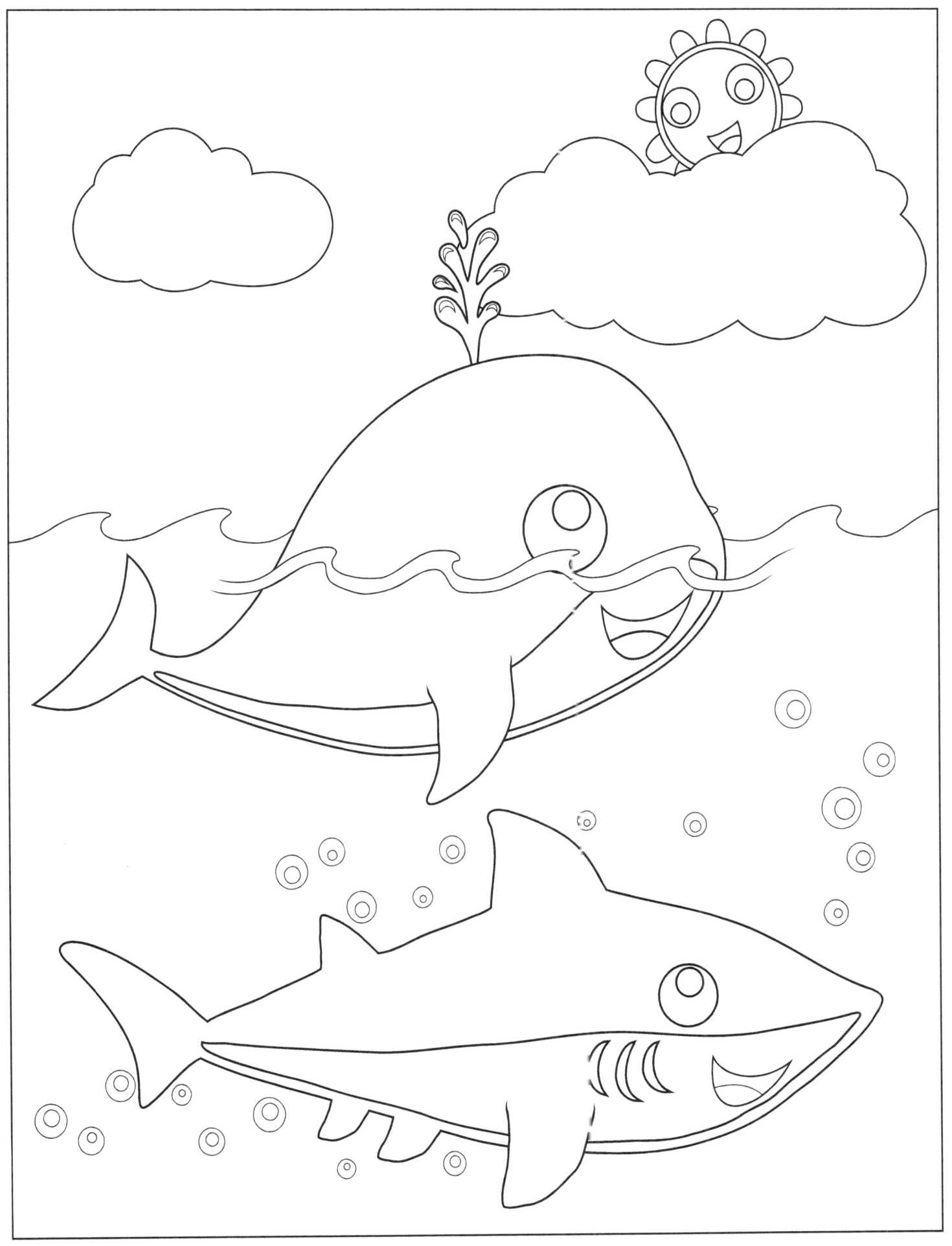

www.ingramcontent.com/pod-product-compliance
Lightning Source LLC
Chambersburg PA
CBHW080516220526
45465CB00006B/2505